A Spot Supremely Blest

This book is reverently and lovingly dedicated
to the memory of my late father,

John Young

And to Cathryn and Rachael, the two granddaughters he never knew.

Front cover: Langholm from the Velvet Knowe
Rear cover: A winter frost by the Roon' Hoose

A Spot Supremely Blest

THE HISTORY, LORE AND LEGENDS OF LANGHOLM

W S Young

ISBN 0 9517858 3 4

First Edition 2004

Printed by Buccleuch Printers, Carnarvon Street, Hawick TD9 7EB
www.buccleuchprinters.co.uk

Published by Cairndhu Publishing, Walter Street, Langholm DG13 0AX
www.cairndhu.net

Books produced by Cairndhu Publications

The Railway to Langholm   *ISBN 0 9517858 0 X*

The Ewes Valley   *ISBN 0 9517858 1 2*

Memorial Inscriptions of Langholm Old, Staplegordon and Wauchope Churchyards   *ISBN 0 9517858 2 6*

Contents

The author on Solway ~ Common Riding 1984

Foreword

A *Spot Supremely Blest* is a book about Langholm, compiled by my fellow Langholmite and good friend, Billy Young. The appropriate title of this book is a line taken from the late Matthew Ewart's poem, *A Wee Bit Toon*, later set to music and often sung by popular request on many an occasion by Billy himself.

To the reader, the researcher, the historian and the critic, local or outwith the town, and to any of our younger sons of Eskdale who are interested in all aspects of Langholm, past and present, I would recommend this book.

It is no understatement to say that Billy has left no stone unturned in his meticulous research. What is immediately apparent in his book is the love and dedication the author has for his subject.

The book traces the history of Langholm from its inauspicious beginnings. Billy's book takes us through the centuries and traces the life and times of some notable local characters, Langholmites of stature and achievement who once roamed the hills around oor ain "Wee Bit Toon" before moving further afield to make their mark on the world stage.

From a few simple dwellings on the banks of the Esk, the town grew to a thriving populace of over four thousand inhabitants in the late nineteenth century, Langholm deservedly acquired the worthy title, "The Muckle Toon o' the Langholm".

In Billy's book, we are given a detailed insight of what life was like in our town in the distant past, but we are also brought up-to-date with our present way of life which we sometimes take for granted.

Perhaps by reading this book, the "interlouper" (no disrespect intended) may at last begin to understand that the pride we feel for our birthplace, the spirit of Eskdale that runs in our veins, and the emotion that manifests itself so sincerely on Langholm's great day, is only the natural consequence that comes from living in A SPOT SUPREMELY BLEST.

John G Elliot

An old sketch of Langholm Town Hall and Market Place, between 1842 and 1862,
before Admiral Sir Pulteney Malcolm's statue was re-sited in the Library Gardens.
The King's Arms Inn, with Telford's arch-way, is on the extreme right.
A Mail Coach is entering the Market Place through 'The Straits'.

Introduction

'God gave all men all earth to love,
But, since our hearts are small,
Ordained for each one spot should prove,
Beloved over all.'

Rudyard Kipling

To her sons and daughters scattered throughout the world, Langholm will remain forever their Alpha and their Omega, for neither distance nor the passage of time can lessen the grip that binds 'This Wee Bit Toon' to the hearts of her people.

The exile, who is cast upon some foreign shore, will often wander back in his mind's eye to the golden days of youth; tae dookin' in the Wauchope water or sledging on the foothills o' Whita, tae the laughter, fun and fellowship that pervaded the Langholm of his youth. The longing to revisit these 'dear auld haunts o' hame': tae hear yince mair the jow o' the Toon Hall clock or the sweet music of his mither tongue, to walk his beloved hills and hear the plaintive cry o' the curlew, these images call to him across the years as his heart aches for the only place he will ever call home.

Whenever Langholmites meet in some far-off clime, be it in the wide expanses of Africa or in the hustle and bustle of one of America's great cities, little time passes before the 'crack' turns inevitably to thoughts o' hame, to 'weel kent faces' and the cherished scenes of the past and, ignoring the glories around them, they prefer, instead, to bask in the warm and comforting glow of nostalgia.

It is all too easy to over-glorify one's native town. Langholm is not Brigadoon, that mythical and magical Highland village that was locked forever in the past. In recent years, the town has suffered the same hardships that every Border town has suffered: the drastic decline in our staple industry – textiles, and gradual depopulation as the young leave in search of better opportunities or a higher education. However, no one should underestimate the resilience of Langholm people, for are we not descendants of the most skilful and determined fighters in Europe – the Border Reivers? This town, which once depended entirely on the production of high-class cloths for its prosperity, has been forced to change its strategy by diversifying into other fields. The town has begun to market the rich heritage and beauty that is around us, but which we so often take for granted.

We each have a story to tell. Some stories are sad, some inspiring and others mundane. Langholm's story is the sum total of all the stories its people have told down the ages.

It is the tale of a settlement, which probably grew up round a fortification during a time of unrivalled terror and violence, and which, by local expertise and by sheer dint of hard work, became a world-renowned centre of excellence for the production of fine cloths. Its famous sons have left their marks in many different spheres, as entrepreneurs, soldiers, statesmen, ambassadors, writers, poets and engineers. One descendant of a local clan stands proud as one of the greatest explorers of all time. The town's Common Riding can rightly claim to be one of the finest people's festivals of Britain, if not of Europe, rivalling even Sienna or the Bull Festival of Pamplona. Langholm has so much to offer, not least of which is the soaring spirit of its people, for their dogged determination to succeed against all hardship and adversity, unaided: this 'ersitness' has been the key to its success over the centuries.

The origins of this book go back to a rash moment in 1994 when the author accepted an invitation to speak on Langholm at the Selkirkshire Antiquarian Society. Being armed with a marvellous collection of old slides, he naively thought that all that was required was to quickly skim through the last 550 years of local history.

This task, which he thought he would complete in a couple of weeks, has taken ten years, and has culminated in the production of this book.

A Spot Supremely Blest is not intended to compete with the two local 'Bibles' *Langholm As It Was* (first published in 1912) or *Lang Syne In Eskdale* (published in 1950) for they stand alone as supreme sources of local knowledge. Rather, it is written to supplement these great works, by bringing the story of Langholm right up to the present day.

The author offers no apology for using local words and phrases, as he hopes this may encourage their survival. If this book inspires a future generation to cherish the customs and heritage of Langholm, and to strive to retain its unique character, then it will have achieved all it set out to achieve.

William S Young
Langholm

June 2004

Acknowledgements

In writing this book, the author gratefully acknowledges the great help and support that many have given him.

He would like to extend his sincere thanks to the publisher, Mr Bruce McCartney for his skill and patience in setting out this book, to Mr Arthur Bell and Mr Alex MacCracken for sharing their extensive local knowledge with him, to Mr Billy Ewart and Mr Alec Borthwick for contributing their excellent artwork, to Mr John Elliot (Hallpath) for his Foreword and to the proof readers, Miss Brenda Morrison, Mrs Lesley McBay, Mrs Violet Graham, Mrs Grace Baxter, Mrs Lesley McCartney and Mrs Liz Young.

The author is also very indebted to the following, who lent him books, articles, photographs for reproduction, or who have willingly offered information.

Reid & Taylor Ltd, Carcanet Press Ltd, The Edinburgh Woollen Mill Ltd, Border Fine Arts Ltd, Langholm Library Trust, The Robert D Clapperton Photographic Trust (Selkirk), Mr David Gordon of Buccleuch Printers (Hawick), The Langholm Culture and Heritage Committee, Cumbria Institution of the Arts, The Institution of Civil Engineers (London), Historic Scotland, Mr Stuart Allan of The National War Museum, The National Library of Scotland, The Clan Armstrong Trust, the Eskdale and Liddesdale Advertiser, the Brethren of Lodge Eskdale Kilwinning, The Ladies of the County Library (Langholm Branch), The Ewart Library (Dumfries), Dr Mike Morgan and Mrs Anne Westgarth of the PHLS (Carlisle), Mrs Deirdre Grieve, Dr Ruth McQuillan, Dr Tom Scott, the late Mr Matt Armstrong, Mr Norman Allan, Mr John Beattie, Miss Brenda Morrison, Mr David Irving, The Fair Crier - Mr Rae Elliot, Major Jim Webber (Deal), Mrs Alison Webber (Alford), The Rev Jimmy Beverley (Texas, USA), Miss Grace Brown, Mrs Betty Little, Mrs Isobel Connelly, Mr Craig Bell, Mr & Mrs Christie Elliot, Mr & Mrs Zander Turnbull, Mr & Mrs Alec Graham, Mr Francis Fitzpatrick, Mr & Mrs Ian Ritchie, Dr Tom Kennedy, Mr John Smith, Mr Jock Scott, Miss Alison Little, Miss Jilly McCord, Latimer's of Langholm, Mr Andrew Scott, Mr Sandy Gill, Mr Drew Weatherstone, Mr David Calvert, Mr Alistair Beckett, Mr Ian Landles (Hawick), Mr Ian Scott (Hawick), the late Mr Vic Tokely (Hawick), Mr Steven Turk, Mr William Steele, Mr Hector Barnfather, Mr Edwin Armitage, Mr Fred Richards, Mr David Stevenson, Mr John Elliot (Whitaside), Mrs Margaret Sanderson, Mr John Murray, Mr Alec Drysdale (Gilnockie), the late Mrs Jean Little, Mrs Vivien Telford-Cole, Miss May George, Mrs Verney Bell, Mrs Alison Hutton, the late Mrs Isa Calvert, Mr Arthur Tolson, Mrs Sheena Gair, Mr Gordon Reid, Mr Leslie Murray, Mr Douglas Harkness, Mr Alan Harvey (London).

And to Liz for her immense patience and understanding.

'There's a spot supremely blest,
Sweeter spot than all the rest,
It's a wee bit toon
That lies near Whita hill.'

Matthew Ewart

🙰 *The Battle of Arkinholm* 🙵

There is a line in a song from a famous American musical that goes "Let's start at the very beginning, a very good place to start ..." which is all very well if you know where the beginning is ...! However, as you travel back through the mists of time to an age before reliable records were kept, it becomes very difficult to pin point exactly when a community came into being. What we do know is that Langholm, the settlement that grew up on the 'lang holm' on the east bank of the Esk, was built on the site of the Battle of Arkinholm, which took place on 1st May 1455. This decisive battle finally broke the power of the great Douglas clan in Eskdale.

On one side were Archibald, Earl of Moray, Hugh, Earl of Ormond and Sir John, Lord of Balveny, all brothers of James, Earl of Douglas, known as the Black Douglas, who was hiding in England at the time. All were the great grandsons of Archibald, 'the grim' Douglas, the most powerful man in Scotland save for the king himself. He owned most of Eskdale, which he ruled from his castle, probably the old baronial castle of Barntalloch at Staplegordon. His son and heir was even less well thought of by his enemies. This Archibald was known as 'the tineman, the loser of battles, (and presumably due to the fact that he had lost part of his 'manhood' in battle and was unable to sire bairns) the man of the unlit lamp and the ungirt (that is, feeble) loins'! After his death the title finally fell, in a convoluted way, to William, eighth Earl of Douglas the son of the bloated seventh Earl, James, 'the gross'. The eighth Earl met his end in King James II's antechamber at Stirling Castle when the king took exception to something he said and, in a fury, stabbed him in the neck! After this the title went to his brother James, nineth and last Earl of Douglas.

In the other corner of the ring that day was George Douglas, fourth Earl of Angus (known as the Red Douglas), who had the support of the king and many border chieftains. On the day of the battle, it is said that the River Esk ran red with the blood of those who fell on the 'lang holm'.

> *'Some hunner years hae come an' gane –*
> *It's a story few can tell-*
> *Sin' a thousand men were hack't an' slain,*
> *An' besides the man wha fell,*
> *There was mony a chiel gaed hiplin' hame*
> *Wi a dawlin' leg or a rippit wame,*
> *Frae the battle o' Arkinwohm.*

Earl Douglas grew sae prood an' great
He'd gie the king a fa;
But when at Abercorn they met,
He cowed and slunk awa-
An' ower the border he fled fast
An' syne cam' back tae fight at last
The battle o' Arkinwohm.

There was Sim o' the Hagg an' Ringan's Tam,
An' Sandie o' Rowanburn an' Yeddie the Pecket,
Wha dee'd in a dawm,
For gie'en Carmichael a turn.
There was Eckie o' Harelaw an' Dickie the Cow,
A' Elliots an' Armstrangs, ripe for a row,
At the battle o' Arkinwohm.'

(This long, rambling poem of over two hundred lines was written by the local worthy 'Auld Tibbie – The Queen' over two hundred years ago.)

The Red Douglas and his allies won the day. Of the trio of brothers who fought for the Black Douglas, Moray was slain in battle, Ormond was wounded and taken prisoner while Balveny fled to England to join his brother in hiding, but eight years later was captured in Eskdale and taken to Edinburgh and beheaded. At a meeting of the Scottish Parliament in June 1455 the Earl, along with his mother and brother were declared traitors and their lands were forfeited to the Crown. As thanks for the part they played in the victory, the king gifted some of these forfeited lands in Eskdale to the chiefs of those clans who had supported him. This act led to the rise of many of the families who still live in this valley, Scotts, Beatties, Glendinnings, Maxwells, Johnstones and, of course: –

'Armstrongs and Elliots! You know where they were bred –
Above the dancing mountain burns, among the misty scaurs;
And through their veins, these Border lads, the raiding blood runs red
The blood that's out before the dawn and home behind the stars!'

From 'A Border Toast'
W H Ogilvie

Langholm Castle

 ## & the Reiving Days

The name Langholm first appeared in text in a Kelso Charter dated 1249. Very little is recorded about Eskdale and its environs during the next two hundred and fifty years.

Up until 1793, one of the oldest structures in or near Langholm was a medieval packhorse bridge, which spanned the Wauchope Water at the Auld Caul, just below the Manse. This bridge lay on the line of the Roman Road from Broomholm to Birrens, and crossed the river at the point where a wooden Roman bridge had been, many centuries before. It is ironic to think that the Minister, the Rev Thomas Martin, had it demolished for no better reason than to prevent young boys from the town loitering there on summer nights, so distracting his young servant girls from their devotions.

Today the oldest building, or remains of a building, in the area is the broken down corner on the Castleholm that was once Langholm Castle. Its history is intertwined with those of two of the most prominent riding families on the border, the Armstrongs and Maxwells. Sir William de Coninburcht first granted the lands on which the castle was built to Herbert de Maxwell in 1266. After falling into the hands of the Lindsays and then the Earls of Douglas, they were gifted to the Earls of Angus after the battle of Arkinholm. They were then handed back, once again, to the Maxwell family. However, the Maxwells 'blotted their copybook' once too often, and they were finally handed over to the Earls of Buccleuch in 1643.

By 1500, the Armstrongs had started to spill out of their traditional lands in Liddesdale and had begun to colonise the surrounding valleys of Eskdale, Ewesdale, and Annandale. Pressure of population was one contributing factor. However, at that time the Scottish Crown was actively encouraging men of a certain status to build defensive towers in, or along the edge of, the Debatable Lands. Building a tower within the Debatable Lands was a shrewd move, as neither Scotland nor England would allow the other side to expel a family from such a building as this would automatically imply that that side had accepted responsibility over this 'nest of vipers'.

In 1525, Robert, fifth Lord Maxwell and Warden of the West Marches of Scotland, granted a charter to Johnnie Armstrong of Langholm (or Langhope), a brother of the Laird of Mangerton, making him a tenant under free heritage for the lands of "Langholm, Dalbetht, Shield, Dowblane, Staplegorton, and Teviotshields".

Most historians agree that Langholm Castle was built by Christopher Armstrong, Johnnie's brother, in or around 1526. Having received from Lord Maxwell, lands which lay between the rivers Esk and Sark, at a place known as Barngleish, he built a second tower there. Its remains lie beneath the existing farmhouse, which bears the same name.

The remains of Langholm Castle

Langholm Castle was built in a strategic position, on a flat, fertile plain near the confluence of three river valleys. Being built where the rivers Ewes and Esk meet, it guarded the strategic routes north up these river valleys. As a military building, it had a greater importance than the Peel Towers and Bastles of the area, but was inferior to the imposing fortress of Hermitage, which played a major role in the defence of the Western Marches. The castle was never intended to be anyone's personal stronghold. From the outset, it was designed to house a captain (or keeper) and a small garrison of men. Their job was to police Eskdale, and help the Warden to maintain law and order.

Langholm Castle was still inhabited two hundred years later in 1726. Records show that the marriage of James Pasley of Craig and Magdalen, the daughter of Mr Elliot, Chamberlain to the Duke of Buccleuch, took place there. The castle was partially demolished soon after this probably to supply stone to build a new "Bow" (residence) for the Duke's Chamberlain. It has been suggested that this Bow was Langholm Lodge, the summer residence and hunting lodge of the Buccleuch family. *The Statistical Account for 1793* mentions that "this handsome mansion (Langholm Lodge) was finished about three years ago" (some sixty years after the castle was demolished!) and was built from "fine white free-stone, from Langholm Hill, of remarkable durability". In fact, it was the renowned Scottish Architect, James Playfair, credited with designing the County Hall at Forfar and Melville Castle, who built the mansion over the period from 1786-89.

A short, but tantalising, entry in a book entitled *Westerkirk Parish Historical Notes* under the heading 'George Wilson Papers' reads, "1723-28 – Langholm old castle was demolished and a new one built". Unfortunately, these facts serve only to 'muddy the waters'.

A second tower or substantial dwelling once existed in the area situated at that spot at the 'toonfit' where the Buccleuch Arms Hotel (previously called The Salutation Inn) once stood. Indeed old Ordnance Survey maps of the town, like that of 1899, clearly show the "remains of a tower" at this position. An old guidebook to Langholm, written in 1901, refers to this area as the site of the "Ancient Tower of Langholm". This rectangular building, complete with arrow or ventilation slits in its walls, is thought to have been built by the Armstrongs at the beginning of the eighteenth century. The vaulted basement measured 14ft 5ins by 12ft 5ins and had walls 2ft 9ins thick. A stone spiral staircase or turnpike led from the ground to the upper floors. It became incorporated into what is now Buccleuch House. Sadly, this south west wing had to be demolished in 1947 to improve the sightlines of motorists in the area as it jutted out dangerously onto the road. It may well be that the Chamberlain's Bow was, in fact, this new, comfortable townhouse.

Langholm Castle was witness to some of the most daring and dastardly deeds in Border history. It fell into English hands in 1544, during that period in Scottish history known as 'The Rough Wooing', when Thomas, Lord Wharton stormed Dumfriesshire and ransacked much of Eskdale. By this time, the Armstrongs had turned their backs on Scotland and had sworn allegiance to the English throne. This reversal of loyalty, which was so characteristic of them, might have been triggered by the events that took place at Carlenrig in 1530. It may well have been Armstrongs who laid siege to the castle before handing it over to their English Lords. The castle remained in English hands for three years until the Regent, Arran, decided to retake it in July 1547. A messenger was sent throughout the kingdom charging all manner of men to meet him at Peebles before marching south against "the Langhope and its rebels". Those who failed to turn up, and there were many, were branded traitors and had their property confiscated! The expedition south appears to have been on a grand scale, and was backed up with a fearsome array of hardware including a single falcon, two double-falcons and a medium culverine along with pavilions, munitions etc. After the Scottish artillery fired seven shots into the upper floors of the castle, the besieged English surrendered and were sent home ... "tae think again"!

For most of the sixteenth century, the castle lay at the centre of a custody battle between the Maxwells and other border clans, as the fortunes of this great Border family waxed and waned.

By 1581, it was back in the hands of John, eighth Lord Maxwell who had regained the title Lord Warden of the West Marches from his mortal enemy, John Johnstone of that ilk. In September of that year, Christie Armstrong of Barngleish, and a band of Scottish desperadoes from across the border, attacked the castle, burnt all the furnishings and imprisoned its captain, Herbert Maxwell. That same year the Earl of Angus, who harboured an intense hatred of Maxwell, had all his lands in the area forfeited because of his support for the late Regent, Morton. When the vacant Earldom of Morton was offered to Maxwell this proved to be 'the straw which broke the camel's back'. Angus vented his wrath by attacking the castle early in 1582, but failed to take it. After much 'toing and froing' the castle was back in Maxwell's hands by 1585.

However, Maxwell's luck was beginning to change again. In 1587, he incurred the wrath of King James VI by travelling to Spain to help plan a Spanish invasion of England through Scotland. The normally timid King retorted by sending an army to destroy all of Maxwell's strongholds. The castle was set on fire and Maxwell was taken prisoner.

After another upturn in his fortunes, this 'India rubber man' was released and re-instated as Warden in 1592. The following year he met his nemesis at the Battle of Dryfe Sands, the last clan battle to be fought on the border. He was knocked from his horse, and being weighed down with armour, could not get onto his feet again. What happened next is pure conjecture; according to one account he was 'brained' by the wife of Johnstone of Kirkhill using the tower keys that hung from her girdle. Willy Johnstone then unceremoniously cut off his arm, before taking it as a trophy and nailing it to the wall at Lochwood Castle.

After this, Langholm Castle was referred to in state papers as one of his Majesty's 'oun houses'. The building was probably still Maxwell property, although when required was to be handed over to the State.

On the 24th March 1603 Sir Robert Carey, Warden of the English Middle March, embarked on a remarkable journey north from the English Court to Holyrood. He covered the 400-mile journey in the space of sixty hours, on a relay of post horses. What made this feat all the more remarkable was the fact that he was thrown from his horse somewhere in Berwickshire, and lay concussed for some time after being kicked in the head! He carried two things with him on his epic journey.

One was the news that the old Queen, Elizabeth I, was dead; the other was the coronation ring, which his sister, Philadelphia, had taken from the dead Queen's finger. This ring, a gift from James VI of Scotland, was to convince the Scots King, if proof were needed, that he now ruled over two kingdoms. The King was asleep by the time Carey's horse clattered into the courtyard late on the Saturday night. He was immediately admitted to the royal bedchamber, where he knelt to salute the new King of England. That frantic ride heralded the end of a way of life on the border that had endured for centuries. The borderland was about to experience peace for the first time since 1286!

Langholm Castle was hammered for the last time when James, on his way south to claim the English throne, paused at Berwick to dispatch Sir William Selby with 1,000 horse and 200 footmen to execute marauders and blow up their houses in

Liddesdale and Eskdale. This parting gift was his brutal response to the efforts of broken clans to keep the kingdoms divided (and ablaze!) during those few crazy days – known as 'the Ill or Busy Week' – following the Queen's death. A tradition existed that all laws in a kingdom were suspended in the period between the death of one monarch and the proclamation of his successor. The Border clans sensed that James's accession to the English throne might mean the end of these 'good old days' and resolved to go on one last 'feeding frenzy'. In that short space of time every desperado who could still throw his leg over a horse was mounted, and had crossed into England to wreak havoc. The Grahams, Elliots and Armstrongs launched full-scale attacks on Cumbria and came home with more than 5,000 head of cattle.

The new King's response to this was completely disproportionate. The Graham clan was singled out for particular attention; those who were not hanged by the absurd process known as 'Jedart Justice' (where the accused was hanged first and tried later!) fled abroad or were deported to Ireland. In Liddesdale the great Armstrong clan was all but annihilated, many ending their days on a hanging tree or at the bottom of a mountain burn. Three thousand Elliots are thought to have fled from the region.

Eskdale fared better than most, for when the 'hounds arrived to harry the hares' they had already fled to their famous bolthole on the Tarras Moss to regroup and consider their next move.

Billy Ewart's impression of Langholm Castle

The broken-down corner of the castle that exists today gives no indication of the scale of the building or what it looked like. The Platte of Castlemilk, which was prepared for Lord Wharton shortly after the Scottish siege of 1547, shows it to be a stocky tower-like building, which was surmounted by a turret or cap-house. Soldiers would not have been billeted in the main tower itself, but rather in lower, unfortified buildings on either side of it called 'Laich Houses', which also acted as byres and stables!

The present ruin is thought to be a fragment from the south end of the main tower. This might have been built (or rebuilt) after the siege of 1547 when, we are told, the English garrison within the castle destroyed the lower part of the building. The rough ground on three sides suggests outbuildings once existed, while earthworks to the southwest may be the remains of a moat. More often than not moats were dry structures, the rationale for this being that it was possible to float or swim across a water-filled moat unnoticed, whereas it was almost impossible to traverse a deep, dry moat without being seen or heard. The sketch by local artist Billy Ewart is based on a map of the area made in 1775 and from recent data gleaned from dowsing studies and observations of the visible remains. It shows the imposing main tower of Langholm Castle, flanked on two sides by longer and lower 'Laich Houses'.

The stone used to build the castle was cut from the quarries on Whita Hill; and this local tradition of building with Whita sandstone continued from then until about 1935, when these quarries finally closed.

The Famous Armstrong Clan

The most colourful episodes in Langholm Castle's history concern its involvement with two famous members of the Armstrong clan.

It was here that Johnnie Armstrong and his "gallant cumpanie, ran their horse and brak their spears" (jousted) before riding out to meet their king, James V, in July 1530. Johnnie was without doubt one of the most charismatic of all Border characters and holds a unique place in the folklore of the Borderland.

The ancient kirkyard at Carlenrig, between Langholm and Hawick, is as renowned in Border history as are the battlefields of Flodden and Otterburn. For it was here that the boy-king James finally rid himself of an outlaw who had been such a massive thorn in his side. The king, with between eight and twelve thousand men in attendance, lured Johnnie into a trap by writing him a 'luving letter' in which he promised him a good day's hunting. Johnnie and his men, assuming some kind of safe conduct to be in place, rode north from Langholm dressed in their finest clothes. However, it soon became clear what, or rather who, was being hunted that day, for the party was ambushed at the head of the Ewes valley and Johnnie was brought before his king as a prisoner, rather than as an honoured guest. He tried in vain to reason, but all his pledges of loyalty or offers of riches fell on deaf royal ears …

> *'Grant me my life, my liege, my King!*
> *And a great, great gift I'll gie tae thee –*
> *Bauld four-and-twenty sister's sons*
> *Sall for thee fecht, tho' a' should flee!*
>
> *Away, away thou traitor strang!*
> *Out o' my sight soon mayst thou be!*
> *I grantit never a traitor's life*
> *And now I'll not begin wi' thee.'*

Anon

'Blak Jok's' reign on the Border had reached its end. No amount of pleading could delay the inevitable, as the noose began to tighten round his neck.

> *'To seik het water beneith cauld ice,*
> *Surely it is a greit follie –*
> *I have ask'd grace at a graceless face,*
> *But there is nane for my men and me!'*

Anon

Johnnie and his men were summarily hanged upon the 'growand trees' at Carlenrig, without being given even the most basic trial. Sandie Scott however was burned alive because he was accused of burning a poor widow's house, along with some of her children! The trees on which the king's captives were hanged were said to have withered away and died, as if unable to accept the part they were forced to play in this terrible act.

Johnnie Armstrong's memorial
in Teviothead Churchyard, near Carlenrig

> '*Where rising Teviot joins the Frostylee*
> *Stands the huge trunk of many a leafless tree.*
> *No verdant woodbine wreaths their age adorn;*
> *Bare are the boughs, the gnarled roots uptorn.*
> *Here shone no sunbeam, fell no summer-dew,*
> *Nor ever grass beneath the branches grew,*
> *Since that bold chief who Henry's power defied,*
> *True to his country, as a traitor died.*'
>
> From Leyden's 'Scenes of Infancy'

Days after the massacre, Armstrong's estates were gifted by the king to Robert, Lord Maxwell who, possibly, had played a part in this terrible act of treachery. However, Maxwell, along with the Lord of Home, the Lairds of Buccleuch, Ferniehirst and Johnston, was securely warded in Edinburgh Castle at the time to prevent any unwanted intervention.

From Carlenrig the king and his retinue moved to Priesthaugh on Allan Water where he had arranged to meet representatives of the Elliot family. The Elliots, however, declined his invitation!

A legend tells that one of Johnnie's brothers, Archie of Mangerton, managed to escape the carnage. Gathering what was left of his family, he fled to a safe haven on the Tarras Moss by using the secret routes through this treacherous bog that were known only to the freebooters. When the king's men arrived at Gilnockie Tower, they found it deserted. One member of the party was determined to have one of Johnnie's horses as a trophy of their victory over him. When he mounted it, however, it took off at lightning speed toward the Moss, as he tried in vain to control it! It is said that it went right to the place where Archie and his family were hiding, and, as it galloped into the camp, Archie who was busy cutting wood to build a fire, killed the man with a single blow from his axe!

The existing tower, known locally as Hollows or Gilnockie Tower, was always thought to be the home of Johnnie Armstrong; however some feel the weight of evidence suggests that Gilnockie's Tower was not sited here at all! Their preferred site, on the east bank of the Esk near to where Gilnockie Bridge spans the river today, is on a projecting spur of rock which rises on two sides almost vertically out of the water some sixty feet below. They suggest that the reason for there being no visible remains is that the stone from it was used to build this bridge in 1789. At the same time, it has to be argued that some vestiges of rough stones and mortar from the walls must surely have been left at the site. Excavations have failed to uncover the slightest trace of any kind of masonry. It has been suggested that the earthworks, which do exist at this prime strategic position, belonged to a much earlier twelfth or thirteenth century timber castle, such as Liddell Castle or Liddell Strength, or are Roman remains. The question as to where Johnnie's tower was may never be completely resolved.

If the massacre at Carlenrig were the blackest deed to befall the West Marches during the sixteenth century, then the events of March 1596 were, in complete contrast, the most shining and heroic. In that year 'the boot was on the other foot' – for at a race meeting (or perhaps a football game?) at Langholm Castle, 'the Bold Buccleuch' and other border chieftains plotted a daring raid to release the freebooter Kinmont Willie Armstrong from imprisonment in Carlisle Castle. Salkeld the deputy to Lord Scrope, the English Warden, had wrongfully arrested

Hollows or Gilnockie Tower

Kinmont during a day of truce at the Dayholme of Kershope on the banks of the Liddel. By violating the truce-day law (which stated that anyone attending such meetings was immune from arrest until the next sunrise), Scrope had infuriated young Walter Scott of Buccleuch, the Keeper of Liddesdale. So, with a small band of handpicked men Scott set out one night under the cover of darkness to 'herry a corbie's nest' and set Kinmont free.

The numbers involved vary from one account to another: Buccleuch's own reckoning was 80, while Scrope's estimate was 500 – which seems a little fanciful. The ballad sets the number at 40, and, as the element of stealth would be imperative to such an operation, this or at most 80 seems a more plausible number.

Buccleuch picked only the best. The party was made up of Scotts, Elliots and of course Armstrongs and included such famous locals as Walter Scott (Auld Wat) o' Harden, Kinmont's four sons, Walter Scott of Goldielands, John Elliot of Copshaw, Armstrong, the Laird of Mangerton, Armstrong, the young Laird of Whithaugh, young John Armstrong of the Hollows, Christie Armstrong of Barngleish, Roby of

Langholm, Willie Kang Irvine, Jocke Armstrong of the Bighames and one Ally ...
a bastard!

> 'And have they ta'en him, Kinmont Willie,
> Withouten neither dread or fear?
> And forgotten that the Bauld Buccleuch
> Can back a steed, or shake a spear?
>
> I would set that castell in a lowe
> And sloken it with English blood !
> There's never a man in Cumberland,
> Should ken where Carlisle castell stood.
>
> But since nae war's between the lands,
> And there is peace, and peace should be;
> I'll neither harm English lad or lass,
> And yet the Kinmont shall be free!'

Anon

With the help of spies within the castle, they undermined an oak Postern gate (or had it opened from within!) in the outer corner of the fortification. It was a particularly black and stormy night so the usual guard had taken shelter indoors, or had been warned in advance to 'lie low'. The ballad paints a gallant picture of Kinmont being found in shackles, and then being carried out of the castle on the back of a sturdy reiver named Red Rowan. Unfortunately, the truth is far less colourful. In all probability, he was being held unfettered in a house in the outer bailey of the castle, but still within the confines of its massive outer wall. What is certain is that the whole operation was an 'inside job'. A number of Grahams met and dined with Buccleuch at the races at Langholm Castle on the eve of the raid. They, in turn were in league with Thomas and Lancelot Carleton, both March Officers within the castle. Thomas had been Scrope's Deputy at one time, but had lost this post as Scrope (quite rightly) felt him untrustworthy. These conspirators were able to tell Buccleuch how to get into the castle, and, once inside, where to find Kinmont. He probably knew in advance that a rescue was being planned, and when it would happen. For according to Lord Scrope, a Graham brought Buccleuch's ring to him in prison, and this was to be a sign that his 'deliverance' was at hand.

Once out of the castle, the party headed north as Kinmont bade farewell to the gallows on Harraby Hill where he was to have met his end. The whole operation was minutely planned, with nothing being left to chance. Parties of Irvines and Johnstones were positioned along the way to ambush any English troops who might have pursued Kinmont ... but no one came; they were either too stunned or too embarrassed to show face!

A local legend tells of a cottage on the roadside between Longtown and Langholm called Dick's Tree, which belonged to a blacksmith. He was roused from his bed, just after daybreak, when Buccleuch's lance came crashing in through the window, and he was forced to strike off Kinmont's shackles. Unfortunately, this tale, which has been handed down orally for at least 230 years, has no basis in fact. As he was under house arrest and unshackled, there would have been no need for a blacksmith's services!

This daring raid made young Buccleuch the hero of the day, winning even the admiration of Queen Elizabeth. She is reputed to have asked him "how he dared to undertake an enterprise so desperate and presumptuous?" His arrogant reply was "What is there that a man dare not do?" This so impressed her, that she is reputed to have turned to bystanders and said, "This is a man indeed, with ten thousand such men our brothers in Scotland might shake the firmest throne in Europe".

Exactly 400 years later to the day, in 1996, a cairn was unveiled on the Castleholm at Langholm to commemorate the spot where the raid was planned. That night 'A Border Dinner' was held in a marquee nearby, and was attended by members of many of the clans who were instrumental in Kinmont's release. A toast to 'The Borderland' was eloquently proposed by Ian Landles from Hawick, and drunk using whisky from the cellars of His Grace the Duke of Buccleuch and Queensberry.

In 1987, some members of the Clan Armstrong Trust unearthed an ancient grave slab in Sark Kirkyard. It had been completely covered by turf, but when cleaned it was seen to bear a crude engraving of a left hand and arm (part of the Armstrong crest) with the fingers overlying a saltire. At either end, within two double circles, was a cross pattee (a cross with broad, almost triangular arms). In his *Chronicles of the Armstrongs*, James L Armstrong states "Kinmont lived to a good old age, and was interred in an ancient burying ground near the Tower of Sark". He goes on to say that "the tombstone over his grave had, through time, sunk almost level with the ground, but that a few gentlemen of the name of Armstrong and Graham voluntarily contributed to the expense of remodelling (re-engraving) the tombstone to its ancient form, and that this was accomplished about the year 1800". Could it be that the mortal remains of Kinmont Willie Armstrong (or a son or grandson) lie under this ancient stone, scarcely quarter of a mile from Sark Tower (Morton Rigg), which had been his home?

Before leaving the Armstrong clan, it is worth mentioning another colourful member – Archie Armstrong of the Stubholm. This ancient farm lies at the foot of Warbla Hill, and overlooks that tongue of land that bore the old name Eldingholm, and is now taken up by the Buccleuch Park and the Parish Church grounds.

Archie, the son of Ritchie Armstrong, lived during the reign of James VI and, like his kinsman Johnnie, had a propensity to steal other folk's possessions ... namely their sheep! The story goes that on one occasion he was chased back home by the warden's men, as he carried a sheep he had stolen. He quickly dropped the carcass into the bairn's cradle and happed it up with blankets. When the soldiers burst in, a scene of complete domestic bliss confronted them – the doting father sitting by the fireside rocking his 'bairn' to sleep. When accused of stealing the sheep, he cleverly replied,

> *'If ere I did sae fause a feat*
> *As thine my neighbour's faulds,*
> *May I be doomed the flesh to eat*
> *This very cradle haulds!'*

Anon

As it happened, the hasty deception did not work, for the sheep was found and Archie was marched off to Jedburgh to be tried in front of the king himself. However, on this occasion, his quick-wittedness saved him from the gallows. Indeed the king was so taken by his original brand of pawky wit that he made him his Gentleman Groom, and it was while he held the title that he was made a Freeman of the City of Aberdeen. After that, he was raised to the exalted rank of Court Jester. So, in effect, he became Fool to 'The Wisest Fool in Christendom' and afterwards to his son, King Charles I. As the King's Fool, he grew to become a man of considerable clout at court. As Rigoletto was to discover in Verdi's Opera, a Jester's position can be a precarious one; for the line between making the courtiers laugh and offending them was sometimes only a hair's breadth! It was at the court of Charles I that a bitter vendetta arose between him and Laud, the Archbishop of Canterbury, who had been the butt of many of his jokes. When news reached London of the riot in the High Kirk of Edinburgh when the King tried to impose Laud's Liturgy on the Scottish people, Archie sarcastically asked the Archbishop "Wha's fule now?" (Who's the fool now?) In his fury, Laud had Archie brought before the Privy Council, which decreed on 11th March 1637 that his jester's cap and coat (or motley) should be taken from him and that he should be dismissed from the King's service. So Archie was sent home in disgrace, but the last laugh was on him. When asked by someone what had become of his coat of office he replied, "O, my Lord of Canterbury hath taken it from me, because he or some of his Scotch Bishops may have need of it themselves." Archie Armstrong has gone down in history as the last regular Jester to serve a British Royal household.

Archie was no fool when it came to money, for with his pension from Court, gratuities, and other pickings, he had 'feathered his nest well', buying an estate in Cumberland, and living the rest of his life as a landed gentleman.

> *'Archie, by King and Princes graced of late,*
> *Jested himself into a fair estate.'*

Anon

Archie outlived both Archbishop Laud and King Charles, and was buried at Arthuret near Longtown in March 1672. His grave is unmarked, but is thought to be near to the ancient Cumbrian preaching cross near the centre of the churchyard.

Eskdale during the 'Killing Time'

In May 1685, eighty-nine years after the rescue of Kinmont Willie, John Graham of Claverhouse spent a night at Langholm Castle after playing a part in the murder of the young shepherd boy, Andrew Hislop of Rennaldburn, at Craighaugh. Hislop's only crime was that his widowed mother had sheltered a dying Covenanter in her cottage, and the family later buried his body in a field nearby. However, it was not allowed to lie in peace, for Sir James Johnstone, who was a fierce local persecutor of the Covenanters, discovered it. The Hislop family were soon implicated in the crime, and for this reason had their belongings seized and their house pulled down.

Andrew Hislop was not at home at the time, but was captured by Claverhouse and his men in the parish of Hutton some days later. It is said that he tried to escape on his horse, but that it was flighty, and he was unable to catch it. The locals were asked for a rope to bind him. One woman wrapped her cart rope around her waist and refused to hand it over, but a man came forward with his, saying "I'll give you ropes to hang all the Whigs in Dryfe". Hislop was placed on a horse behind one of the troopers, with his feet tied below the horse's belly. As the troop passed through the village of Boreland, the Blacksmith, Little, rushed out with a red-hot iron and threatened the soldiers if they would not "Louse that bonny man". His feet were untied and the party marched on! Hislop was brought over the hills to Craighaugh and it was here, in the presence of Sir James Johnstone of Westerhall, that he was murdered, shot through the head as he knelt praying. It has been claimed that Claverhouse and his men refused to kill the boy without giving him a fair trial. Hyslop in *Langholm As It Was* suggests it was Sir James Johnstone who finally lost patience and shot the boy himself, but only after Claverhouse yielded, saying: "The blood of this man, Westerhall, be upon you. I am free of it!"

> *'Andrew Hislop, shepherd lad,*
> *'Martyr' graven on thy tomb;*
> *Here you met the brutal Clavers,*
> *Here you bore his murderous doom.*
>
> *So they left you, Martyr brave,*
> *Left you on the reddened sod;*
> *But no raven touched your face*
> *On it lay the peace of God.'*
>
> From Prof Veitch's 'Andrew Hislop, the Martyr'

That night, Claverhouse was the guest of Mr Melville, the Duke's Chamberlain, at the Castle. After much soul searching and anguish he told Mrs Melville that he had been "the butcher of the Government long enough and he would be no longer". That was the last murder in which he ever played a part. As for Westerhall, it is said that he died some time after "in great torture of body and horror and anguish of conscience, in so much that his cries of agony were heard at a great distance from his room when he died".

The Martyr's Grave at Craighaugh

Hislop's mother, on being told of her son's death, said, "It is well it was Andrew, as he was best prepared to die". She insisted on visiting the steading at Craighaugh where he died, and gathered up his brains in a napkin. The local people carried his body from the farm, and buried it in a field nearby. In 1702, they erected a trough tombstone over his grave. Despite attempts by descendants of Johnstone to remove it, it still stands on that grassy slope as a poignant testament to the terrible acts that were, and still are, committed in the name of religion.

John Graham of Claverhouse, or "Bluidy Clavers" as he was known in south-west Scotland, led a strange Jekyll and Hyde existence. As well as being a brutal persecutor of the Covenanters, he was also a loyal and courageous supporter of the Jacobite cause, a supporter of 'the Old Pretender', the erstwhile James VIII – Bonnie Prince Charlie's father. He has been immortalised forever in Sir Walter Scott's famous ballad *Bonnie Dundee*, for his full title was in fact Viscount Dundee. His life ended very dramatically; he was killed by a stray bullet (probably fired by Ringan Oliver, a Border Covenanter) at the Battle of Killiecrankie, just as his men cleared all before them in a terrible and typical Highland charge.

> 'To the Lords of Convention 'twas Claverhouse spoke,
> Ere the King's crown go down there are crowns to be broke,
> So each Cavalier who loves honour and me,
> Let him follow the bonnets of Bonnie Dundee.'

> From 'Bonnie Dundee' by Sir Walter Scott

High up on Timpen Hill, which overlooks the Castleholm, there once grew a wizened old bush known as Cowie's Thorn. Local legend has it that it was near to this spot that another fugitive of these killing times, the preacher Alexander Peden, fled while being pursued by Claverhouse's men. It is said that he prayed to the Almighty to "throw His Godly blanket over them" whereupon a mist miraculously descended upon him and his followers, so hiding them from their pursuers.

There were many in Eskdale who refused to accept the Episcopal form of worship first imposed by King Charles I, continuing, instead, to practise the old forms of Presbyterianism at secret prayer meetings, or conventicles, in these hills.

One famous meeting spot in Eskdale was at Peden's Well, at the base of the small, conical hill known as Peden's View. At this spot, Sandy Peden would preach and christen the children of local Covenanters. It was here that this strange old preacher and seer would utter his prophecies of doom against the murderers of Andrew Hislop – the Johnstones of Westerhall.

During these 'Killing Times', Peden remained a powerful and charismatic force in the South West of Scotland and Ayrshire. As a marked man with a price of 1,000 Merks on his head, he wore an elaborate mask as a disguise to prevent capture but which gave the impression he suffered from some terrible contagious disease. This gun-toting outlaw was said to possess remarkable powers of prophecy. It was during the time that he was imprisoned on the Bass Rock, 'Scotland's Alcatraz for Ministers', that he made his most uncanny prediction. The Governor of the rock was a keen gambler, an activity that Peden thought utterly sinful. He warned that if he did not mend his ways "the Lord would strike him with a wound that would smite him to the very heart"! Soon afterward, the Governor's young daughter died tragically, when a freak wind blew her off the rock and into the sea!

Peden's name also lives on at other places in the Borders; there is a Peden's Pulpit on the slopes of Ruberslaw near Hawick, a Peden's stone at Castleton in Liddesdale and a Peden's Cleuch at Southdean near Jedburgh.

3

The Birth of Langholm

Since earliest times communities have grown up on flat land at the confluence of river valleys. This practice can be traced all the way back to the hunter-gatherers who first colonised the 'wildwood', the vast impenetrable forest which covered the border country after the ice sheets retreated at the end of the eighth millennium. Tribes from the south began to explore this vast forest, but were probably too frightened to probe very far into its dark, mysterious interior on foot. Instead, they sailed up the river valleys from the sea in their dugout canoes or skin boats, and established campsites, which later became settlements, at the confluence of rivers.

Most border towns have grown up where two (or more) rivers meet, and Langholm is no exception. In addition to this, the rough tracks, which mirrored the course of the rivers down these valleys, converged at their confluences, forming a natural road junction or crossroads. If the rivers were shallow enough to be forded here, without the need to build bridges, then all the better. People would tend to gather at these road junctions or river crossings, which meant the opportunity arose to buy or sell; hence they became market places or trading centres. The other factor, which determined where communities grew up, was the issue of protection; settlements often grew up near castles or fortified buildings because of the protection they offered from attack.

Langholm probably started out as a settlement of peasants' huts, which clung to the walls of the castle for protection. In time a symbiotic relationship would develop as the inhabitants of this settlement found they could offer the castle various services, such as the provision of food and fuel, tradesmen, labourers and a ready supply of foot soldiers, in return for the protection it offered them. In old prints of Langholm, like that of Nasmyth (1816), one can see a number of peasant cottages surrounding the ruined fortification. After the Union of the Crowns in 1603, life in the area became more settled as the chance of attack from enemies dwindled. The peasants would then begin to utilise the large plain on the east bank of the Esk, 'the lang holm', on which to build their community. It seems reasonable to assume this is how Langholm, or to give it its older name of Arkinholm, came into being. However, the possibility that a settlement existed here before the castle was built cannot be ruled out for all the sound reasons already given.

In 1608, Lord John Maxwell avenged his father's grisly death by shooting the Chief of the Johnstones twice in the back, before fleeing to France, so ending the bitterest (and bloodiest) feud in British history, which resulted in the death of four clan chiefs and thousands of men.

The following year the king confiscated all of Maxwell's lands in Eskdale and gifted them as a 'free barony' to Lord William Cranstoun in a Charter dated January 1610. Cranstoun, as Deputy Lieutenant of the Scottish Marches, had played a key role in King James's brutal pacification of the Borders. The purging process in 'the Middle Shires' was well under way by the end of 1603, with the hanging of thirty-two Elliots, Armstrongs, Johnstones and Batys (Beatties), while fifteen more were banished and one hindred and forty outlawed. Cranstoun's involvement in acts like these probably won him favour with the king, as well as being granted land in Eskdale.

By 1618, the Maxwells seem to have bounced back into favour, for in this year James started to restore their lands to Robert, tenth Lord Maxwell. Two years later, the king advanced him one step in 'the pecking order' by making him the Earl of Nithsdale.

Langholm as a Burgh of Barony came into being on 19th September 1621 when James VI conferred large amounts of local land, including the Lands of Langholm, on Robert, tenth Lord Maxwell, the Earl of Nithsdale. The term 'Burgh of Barony' refers to a town which falls under the jurisdiction of a local landowner or Baron, the Baron having received certain trading privileges from the Monarch, as laid down in a Royal Charter. This Charter gave the Earl the right to hold weekly markets, two annual fairs (at which he could levy tolls or duties) and to erect a cross in the market place. The cross, a symbol of the Baron's authority, was the point from which all public proclamations were made. He was also required to elect a Baron-Baillie to represent him in all civil and criminal matters. Langholm's first Baillie was John Maxwell of Broomholm, who dispensed justice at the Baron's courts held in the town.

However, on 4th February 1628 the Earl entered into a feu-contract (a heritable lease at a fixed rent) with ten men from his own family in which he gifted each one merkland (a measure of land originally valued at one Merk, Scots) within the lands of Arkinholm, for an annual feu-duty of 25 Merks each. This conveyance made these ten men Langholm's first Burgesses. They were obliged, by this contract, to build "Ilke ane of them a sufficient stone house on the fore street, builded with stone and lyme, of two houses height at the least, containing fourty foots within the walls of length, eighteen foot of breadth, twelve foot of height". The contract went on to state that the street between these houses should be "of thrittie foots of breadth at least". The building of these houses heralded the birth of the town of Langholm. *The Statistical Account for 1793* states that only four houses were actually built. In a footnote in *Langholm As It Was*, Hyslop mentions that George Rome's manuscript states that of these four houses, two were reputed still to be in existence in 1883 on the west side of the High Street near the Douglas Hotel.

Langholm was probably built to the same burgage plot pattern that had been used to build the medieval Scottish towns. The burgesses' properties (the burgage plots or tofts), which lined both sides of the High Street, would consist of their dwellings at the front, with a large strip of land to the rear called the 'backlands'. These backlands housed gardens, outhouses, wells, and middens, and, in time, through pressure for space, housing for the poorer members of the community. These people needed access to the High Street, so 'closes and entries' were built running off it, explaining why the centre of Langholm is riddled with narrow lanes and passages.

The main public building in the town at this time was the Tolbooth or Townhouse. It stood on the spot where the Town Hall stands today, and was replaced by this building in 1811-12. It is not possible to say with any certainty when the Tolbooth was built. The Earl of Nithsdale's Contract of 1628 mentions that a Tolbooth will be built in the High Street, adjacent to the proportion belonging to George Maxwell of Carnsalurth. The building was certainly in existence in 1726 when it was commented that the village of Langholm 'is now very much improven and beautified with a townhouse and prison for the Regality of Eskdale, [and] a cross' and the building served as a meeting place for the Regality and a court for the Justice of the Peace. The old Tolbooth was grim to say the least. It would have been multifunctional, serving as a Courtroom, Market Office, and Gaol. Thomas Telford, in his autobiography, described it as "partly a prison, and partly a justice hall, with an outside stair for ascent. There is a sort of bell tower, which of late years has been furnished with a clock. It occupies the middle of the edifice, and its narrow, iron-grated windows and vault-like entrance give it a gloomy, gaol-like appearance."

The nineteenth century Town Hall was built to Mr Elliot's plan, Mr Elliot probably being William Elliot, a Kelso architect, who was employed by the Duke of

Langholm Town Hall in 1870 before the addition of the Library

Buccleuch at this time. It was built with ashlar from the quarries on Whita Hill, and originally contained three prison cells on the ground floor with the town hall above.

The fine Jacobean style Library was built in 1875-78 on land gifted by the Duke of Buccleuch. It replaced an earlier building, which existed on the south-east side of the Town Hall, and was funded by a donation of £1,000 from Alexander Reid, Manufacturer, and by subscriptions from the proprietary members of the Library. It was proposed that the Town Hall should also be replaced at this time, but this plan never reached fruition.

The Contract of 1628 also identified a sizable area of Common Land within the Burgh. The heritors of the merklands, and their tenants, had the right of free pasture on this Common, and to gather stones from its quarries. Four hundred years later, it is impossible to say where the exact boundaries of Langholm Common were, as they were defined by old place names, which are now unrecognisable, or by changeable objects such as 'a hedge, a dyke, heap of stones or a willow bush'. Suffice to say, the Common almost certainly included all of Whita Hill and some low lying arable ground along the east bank of the Esk above 'Land's End', and covered an area of 750 acres, 2 roods and 36 poles.

Some impression of the state of housing in Langholm during the early part of the 1600s was given by a Cheshire man, named Christopher Lowther, who spent two nights in the town (then only a hamlet) in 1627. He and his two travelling companions spent the first night in a dwelling where the fire was "in the midst of the house". They spent the second night "in a poor thatched house, the wall of it being one course of stones, another of sods of earth (possibly suggesting alternate courses of stones and turf) with a door of wicker rods". What was lacking in the quality of the accommodation was made up for by the hospitality they received, for they were regaled with "mutton, chicken, oatcakes and wheaten bread, washed down with ale and aqua vitae" (whisky).

In January 1883, G R Rome published an excellent lecture, *The History of Eskdale* (which he had first delivered to the London Eskdale Society), in the *Eskdale and Liddesdale Advertiser*. His work gives tantalising glimpses of life in the town from the earliest times. In 1631, he tells that a plague of sturdy Irish beggars infested the area and extorted alms from those who would not give freely. In the end, an order was issued by the Privy Council to clear the country of this nuisance. But in 1644, the area was struck down by a much more deadly pestilence … the plague. It seems the outbreak started in England and gradually spread north: for it was first reported in Newcastle and then later in Edinburgh. For the first time, the city fathers of Edinburgh sent out a physician, Dr Paulitius, to visit victims in their homes. Cleaners were also employed to clean their houses, and to burn all loose thatch and straw.

The terror came in two forms, which was caused by the same bacterium entering the body by different routes. The Bubonic plague was spread by fleas, which lived in the coats of rats, which thrived in these unhygienic conditions. The bodies of the victims became covered with characteristic glandular swellings known as Buboes and by a black discoloration caused by gangrene, hence its more common name – The Black Death. While the even deadlier Pneumonic plague could be transferred from individual to individual by the simple act of sneezing (hence the ominous line in the nursery rhyme, 'Atishoo, atishoo – we all fall down!') and was nearly always fatal. There was also a raft of other terrible diseases such as

Smallpox, Tuberculosis, Measles, Whooping Cough, Rheumatic Fever, Tetanus and Pneumonia, which, along with malnutrition, kept the population in check. With little knowledge of what caused these diseases, and even less knowledge of how to treat them, the population was left at the mercy of charlatans, bleeders, quacks and butchers!

In 1643, the Earl of Nithsdale 'fouled his own nest' through his support for Charles I, and so the Maxwell lands in Eskdale were forfeited for the last time. In that same year, they were passed to Francis, second Earl of Buccleuch, the grandson of 'The Bold Buccleuch'. In this way the House of Buccleuch, which already owned most of Eskdale, inherited the title Lords-superior to the Barony of Langholm.

In Langholm's Charter, the Barons had the right of 'Pit and Gallows', that is to drown in their murder-hole or hang on their private gibbet those malefactors who came under their jurisdiction. Death by drowning was a particularly popular 'method of dispatch' on the Scottish side, and mass drownings were not uncommon. On one occasion a score of reivers were drowned in the Jed, while at Hawick in July 1562, a batch of twenty-two were drowned in the Teviot. It seems that it had one distinct advantage over hanging – it was much cheaper, as a good 'hang raip' (which, of course, could be used only once) cost 8d! Apparently, 'the pit' in Langholm was in the bed of the River Ewes at a place called 'The Grieve', near to the confluence of the Esk and the Ewes. According to Hyslop in *Langholm As It Was*, it was in this drowning pool that Rossie Baittie and her son, William Irving of Auchenrivock, paid the ultimate price and were "drownet in ye said watter to the death" for stealing sixteen sheep.

Eskdale benefited immensely from having the Buccleuch family as Lords-superior. The first Duke of Buccleuch (who before his marriage to Countess Anne had held the title Duke of Monmouth, and was the illegitimate son of King Charles II by Lucy Walter) was responsible for restocking the whole valley after the terrible snowstorm of March 1674, known as 'the thirteen drifty days'. James Hogg, the Ettrick Shepherd, reckoned that only forty young wedders and five ewes survived in a valley capable of sustaining twenty thousand sheep. On one farm all the sheep perished save one black-faced ewe, but she was driven into a loch by a pack of hungry dogs, and drowned! It was the combination of bitingly cold winds and a blizzard of fine, powdery, dry snow, which lasted for thirteen terrible days, that deprived the south of Scotland of nine-tenths of all its sheep. With little warning, and no stock of feedstuffs, farmers resorted to using the carcasses of dead animals to make huge semi-circular walls in order to give those still living some shelter from the unrelenting cold.

Anne was made a Duchess in her own right three years after her marriage to the Duke of Monmouth in 1663. At the king's discretion, she was allowed to retain her titles and lands in Eskdale after her husband's execution, in 1685, for his failed rebellion against King James II. She still holds the unusual distinction of being the only female to inherit the Scott titles and lands in some thirty generations!

In February 1911, The Eskdale and Liddesdale Archaeological Society presented Simon Irving's account of his father's reminiscences to its members. It contained many interesting glimpses of life in the town at the end of the eighteenth century:

"Langholm itself a hundred years ago was a quaint old place, and my father's stories of the old town were very interesting.

The houses were mainly one-storey thatched roof cottages on either side of the straggling street. Where the Crown Hotel now is there was a duck pond called White's Hole. One Frank Beattie built The Crown; my father and he were the first to ride the Common, the custom previously being to walk round the marches.

Before the erection of The Crown, the chief inn was The Caulfield House, which stood in the 'Free Kirk Entry' on the site now occupied by the side entrance to the Hope Hospital. There were a goodly number of inns in Langholm then; the shop and houses occupied by the Misses Cunningham were The Bush; next was The Buck, then came The Crown, then The Commercial; The Globe stood where Mr Giles Latimer's shop now is, The Swan was where Mr Scott's (bookseller) shop is; The Old Cross Keys is now the baker's shop of Mrs Stewart; the present Buccleuch was then known as The Salutation. On the opposite side of the street, the new shop recently opened by Miss Pringle was The George and Dragon, The Royal Oak was the house now occupied by Mr James Harkness, coal agent; The Shoulder of Mutton gave place to The Douglas Hotel; Mr Roddick's (butcher) shop is on the site of The Highland Laddie, The King's Arms occupied the site of the present Temperance (Eskdale) Hotel; The Shepherd's Inn stood where the shop of Mr Beattie (Chemist) now is. I myself can remember the old sign of the inn, the shepherd in his plaid with the dog at his feet".

Simon Irving was born at Townhead, Langholm in September 1833. The house in which he lived was built as a humble thatched cottage by his grandfather, Janetus. In 1822 his father, John converted it into the existing two-storey town house. In addition to running Langholm Mill, the family also had a bakery in premises behind the house. David Irving, the great, great, great, great, great grandson of Janetus Irving, now lives there with his wife and family.

Langholm during 'the 45'

Nineteen ninety five marked the 250th anniversary of a major event in Scottish history, the Jacobite Rebellion of 1745. On 7th November 1745 Prince Charles Edward Stuart and the bulk of his army entered Liddesdale through the Note O' The Gate Pass and stayed at the old Elliot stronghold of Larriston (illustrated right) overnight. Another division of cavalry, consisting of Lord Kilmarnock's and Lord Pitsligo's horse, travelled down through Lauder, Selkirk, Hawick and Langholm. At Spittal-on-Rule some local lads slipped into their camp in the middle of the night and stole the paymaster's money. The Jacobites threatened to burn the village of Denholm to the ground if it was not returned – it was! This division travelled

down the Ewes valley and into Langholm in search of food and fresh horses, and in doing so left two indelible marks on the town – one is the scar a claymore made on the fabric of a building – the other is a local place name.

It is likely that they would have entered the town by way of the old Chapel Path, crossing the Ewes at a ford at Ewes Foot. Their arrival would, no doubt, have been heralded by a lusty skirl on the bagpipes. They made their way along the old Drove Road, then the principal route south through the town, to the farmhouse of John Hounam, which was situated near to Langholm Kirk Yard. Like most Borderers, John had little sympathy for the Stuart cause and took the precaution of driving all his cattle and horses onto the Tarras Moss for safety. When the Jacobite officer demanded that John's wife should tell him where they were hiding their livestock, she refused to do so. In his anger, he threatened to cut down the beam, which supported the roof of the cottage, but still she refused to talk. Being true to his word he drew his claymore and hacked at the beam, which being made of good strong oak, survived the attack. Years later, when this farmhouse was being converted into the existing two-storey house called Mount Hooley, part of the beam bearing the mark of the Highlander's claymore was built as a lintel into a window and is probably still there today under half an inch of wallpaper and plaster.

The claim that Bonnie Prince Charlie watered his horse at Betty's Woll (Well) has no basis in fact, as all records conclusively show that he never visited Langholm! However, the officers who led the division that did enter the town would probably have chosen to stay at The Royal Oak, which was Langholm's premier inn at this time. This old hostelry was sited on the southwest side of 'The Straits', near where the Douglas Hotel stands today. Its stables were very close to this famous old watering hole, so it is conceivable that the horses were taken there after the long ride south from Hawick.

Few men on that epic journey south shared 'The Young Chevalier's' spirit of adventure. One thousand, one fifth of the entire army, deserted during the 100-mile trek from Edinburgh to Carlisle! The conditions they faced were atrocious. Heavy snowfall had made progress very difficult for the bulk of the army, as they had no shoes and were forced to sleep in the open! However, the snow proved to be a mixed blessing as it blocked the road west of Hexham so preventing General Wade from intercepting the Jacobite troops at Carlisle.

During their retreat north from Derby, the bulk of this army forded the flooded Esk at Longtown. They did this by forming ranks of twelve abreast, and interlocked their arms in such a way as to prevent anyone from being swept downstream by the force of the river. Once everyone was safely across, fires were lit and they "danced themselves dry to the pibroch sound". In her song, *The Hundred Pipers*, Lady Nairn, either in error or for poetic licence, places this event during the advance into England.

The only bridge across the Esk, from where it entered the Solway Firth, was the Skippers Bridge (illustrated overleaf), which had been built fifty years before this. In his book *Prince Charlie and the Borderland*, David J Beattie suggests that it is highly likely that the 'baggage' belonging to this army would be transported in carts down the east bank of the swollen Esk, before crossing the river at the Skippers Bridge. From here, the baggage would travel across the old drove road to the Wauchope valley, before meeting up with the rest of the Highland army on

Skippers Bridge

the highway to Glasgow. Beattie also mentions that some clansmen deserted their ranks and found their own way home.

It was while a division of this army was camped at Langholm that the second local incident allegedly occurred.

As this company of Highlanders passed through Langholm and headed north up the old road toward the Ewes valley, scornful words were exchanged between one of their Captains, Bernard Walker, and a local man – old Jimmie Irving. Walker had been garrisoned in Carlisle while the rest of the army marched south, and had visited Langholm regularly during that time. On one of these visits, he had encountered old Jimmie and had grown to despise him. It is hardly surprising that what started out as an exchange of insults between the two men soon flared up into a violent argument. The Captain ordered two soldiers to drag old Jimmie to the edge of a steep bank, and throw him into the deep, swirling pool below if he would not tell them where he had hidden his livestock. This Jimmie vehemently refused to do. In a rage, the Jacobite drew his claymore and advanced on the old man but in doing so accidentally struck his granddaughter, Flora, across the temple with the flat of his sword, knocking her to the ground. At this point her brother, young Jimmie, arrived on the scene and was so incensed by what he saw that he grabbed a sword from one of the soldiers and began to duel with the Captain. Although only a seventeen-year-old boy, young Jimmie had been well taught by his grandfather. After a desperate fight, he finally succeeded in delivering a fatal blow to Walker's side. With their Captain dead, the small band of Highlanders could see that they were outnumbered by townsfolk, and were advised to leave quietly. Young Jimmie and his friends followed them up the road for a few miles to make sure that they were well clear of the town. When they returned they discovered Walker's body floating in the dark waters of the pool below. They were soon at work preparing a deep grave, near the spot where he fell. Walker's body was buried in this unmarked grave, where the modern road twists round this swirling pool in the Ewes River. The only memorial that remains to this man is the name Walker's Hole, but whether this refers to the grave or the pool nearby, no one can say.

The Model Village of 'New Langholm'

Until 1778, the town of Langholm was confined to the land on the east bank of the Esk. However, in that year, the third Duke of Buccleuch, 'The Good Duke Henry', embarked on an ambitious project, which brought about an explosion in the population and heralded the dawn of local industry. Henry built, on land on the west bank of the Esk that once belonged to the farms of Meikleholm and Waas (Walls), his model village of New Langholm. This village, designed by the Duke's Surveyor, was set out in the now familiar grid-iron style with wide criss-crossing streets. It contrasted sharply with the cluttered and irregular layout of the old town, which grew up round the High Street and Drove Road.

About one hundred and forty houses were built over a period of twenty years. The conditions, which the Duke laid down for the building of these houses, probably mirrored those for other houses being built on his land at this time. Namely, the Duke bought the materials required to build the houses, but the tenants, mostly trades people, were expected to haul the materials to the site and pay the building costs, although these costs would be taken into consideration at the end of the 99-year lease. In this way the ordinary working man could dramatically improve his living conditions without using too much of his own capital. *The Statistical Account for 1793* states that single-storey houses came with a field of two acres attached, while two storey houses had four acres of land. These fields, situated along the foot of the surrounding hills, were leased for a period of fourteen years and the annual rent varied from 3/- to 14/- per acre, depending on the quality of the land and its situation. The Staneholm Farm was one such farm, which was broken up to provide stints (an allocation of land) for the tenants of the New Town. The tenants also had common grazing rights on the surrounding hills of Warbla, Meikleholm and Castle Hill, for an annual payment of 18/-. This common pasture was appropriated off the adjoining farms when 'the village' was being built. It occupied the land now taken up by the Langfauld Wood and its ground extended to the road above Langholm Mill.

The Duke also granted his tenants the right to harvest peat (for fuel) from the peat moss on the side of Warbla, and to facilitate this the Peat Road – which still exists – was built.

Among the first cottages to be built in the New Town were those which ran along both sides of Henry Street to Moodlawpoint and on beyond Wauchope Raw (Caroline or Manse Street). On Henry Street, a double row of cottages ran part of the way down each side of the street, with a narrow lane separating the front and back rows. This explains why the width of this street is comparable with the best streets of any other country town.

At the corner where Henry Street and Walter Street now meet was a picturesque high-arched stone brig called the 'The Dam Brig', which spanned the mill dam at the point where it crossed Henry Street. This disappeared in the mid 1880s when work was carried out to cover the open waterway on Walter Street. "But the untiring wheels of time travel on", and it was about this time that demolition of the old cottages was started to make way for the present, substantial terraced houses.

Sadly, almost all of the whitewashed but-and-ben cottages of New Langholm have disappeared, apart from one or two, which are left near Moodlawpoint on Caroline Street.

This same enterprising gentleman, Duke Henry, was also responsible for the birth of another 'model village' in this area – Newcastleton or Copshawholm. For almost 800 years, the people of Liddesdale had lived a reasonably peaceful existence in their community of Castleton on the banks of the Liddel. But in March 1793 the third Duke moved the villagers (some would say evicted them!) from this spot to a 100-acre site on the farm of Park where, under similar conditions to Langholm, he encouraged them to build what he hoped would be a handloom-weaving centre.

In his book, *Liddesdale: Historical and Descriptive*, John Byers (Blue Bell) adopts a more cynical view of why Henry built his model village. "Henry, third Duke of Buccleuch, a highly respected gentleman by all accounts, like other great Scottish landlords at that time, resolved to clear away from his Liddesdale estates the small farms, crofts, cottars' houses and hamlets in order to establish the large sheep farms with which we are familiar today. Before this drastic policy could be carried into effect a definite plan had to be thought out. Since there was no seashore where the people could be dumped, something, however trivial, had to be done for the hundreds of men, women and children who were to be displaced and rendered homeless".

While there may be some truth in the claim that these villages were built to clear people off the Duke's land, no one could possibly argue that the move did not bring about a vast improvement in living conditions for those involved. Comfortable, spacious houses made from local stone, with stone fireplaces and wooden floors quickly replaced the mud and thatch hovels that they were forced to share 'wi the kye or the pig!'

While New Langholm quickly established itself as a thriving centre for the cotton and handloom weaving trade, Newcastleton failed to live up to its expectations as a similar weaving centre, even after the arrival of the railway in July 1862. The relentless march of progress had by-passed this isolated, but beautiful valley. Today Copshawholm is a proud and thriving community with a strong sense of identity. Moreover, while 'the Holm folk' keep one eye on their rich and bloody past, the other gazes optimistically into the future, which promises to be rosier than it has ever been.

4

Religion, the Parish

 # *& the Church*

The annals of the Parish and Auld Kirk of Langholm give a compelling glimpse of Eskdale. Even before the coming of Christianity to the Scottish Borders, the inhabitants of the area were subjected to constant turmoil and fighting with little rest or peace, and this state of affairs continued until the 1745 rebellion.

The first crisis came with the Roman invasion, followed by those of the Saxons and the Danes. The country then suffered during the Wars of Independence when Scotland struggled for its national existence. Eskdale men took part in the battles of Flodden in 1513 and the Solway Moss in 1542. These battles were the outcome of the disconcerting game which Scotland and England played, each conspiring one against the other, with the result that the whole Borderland became the seat of lawlessness and disorder. Arising from this were the Border Reivers whose activities led to still further impoverishment of the countryside. With so much lawlessness and unrest, it is little wonder that the Church had its troubles too, more so during the latter part of the seventeenth century when the Covenanters came into being.

The Girdle Stanes and Loupin' Stanes situated in Eskdalemuir are evidence of religious worship dating back to the year 1290BC. In those very early days the inhabitants of the countryside were sun-worshippers, and it was here, at these stone circles, that the priests carried out their religious activities, and here too, they greeted the rising sun with high festival and great ceremony.

The Romans came over to Britain in 55BC, but it was not until the years 117-138AD that they reached Scotland. It was after that date that the Christian faith began slowly to influence the life of the people. Many of the pagan practices were incorporated in it, and in the seventh century ecclesiastic authorities were still denouncing these practices. Even as late as the eleventh century it was found necessary to restrain the people from worshipping the sun, moon, rivers and hills. However the real source of Scottish Christianity was the Irish Mission on Iona, established by St Columba in the year 523, and which was a Church independent of both Rome and England.

St Patrick was a native of Strathclyde and so had a greater influence in Dumfriesshire than St Columba. Many of the local place names bear this out – Kirkpatrick-Fleming, Kirkpatrick-Juxta, amongst others. In the thirteenth century a fountain known as the Fountain of St Patrick was mentioned in the neighbourhood of Staplegordon, also to St Bridget was dedicated what was probably the earliest church in Eskdale, St Bride's Chapel on St Bride's Hill in Wauchope, not far from the old schoolhouse. Later in time came St Cuthbert, who made a great impression on the early Church in Scotland. Locally, the Over-Kirk of Ewes was dedicated to his memory.

Langholm was originally included in the ancient parish of "Staplegortoun." William de Cunnigburc, who possessed the manor of Staplegortoun in the twelfth century, granted to the Monks of Kelso the Church of Staplegortoun with all the lands belonging to it. The Monks held these lands till the Reformation, when not only Staplegortoun but also several other churches of the Monks were transferred to the Earl of Roxburgh. Some time later the King bought the titles of the parish and in 1637 transferred them to the Bishop of Glasgow.

The Restoration Act was passed in 1662 and this was followed by the Revolution in 1688. This was a nebulous time for Scotland when the minister's home "was the mountain and the wood." The efforts of Charles II to destroy the Presbyterian form of church government in Scotland and introduce Episcopacy in its place were met with the most determined resistance by the Border peoples. The Collation Act of 1662 required all Presbyterian Ministers to submit to re-ordination by a bishop. Rather than accept these conditions, between three hundred and six hundred ministers left their churches one dreary November day in 1662. Of the ten ministers then resident in Eskdale, no fewer than six remained staunch to their convictions and left their churches.

At the time of the Restoration Act, the Rev Robert Law, who remained true to his convictions and left the church, was the incumbent of Staplegortoun. In 1674 he was imprisoned in Glasgow for preaching at conventicles and again in July of the same year, Rev Law was brought before the Civil Court on a charge of preaching in private houses and was forced to enter security for 5,000 merks. Fourteen years later however, after the Revolution, he was finally restored to his church.

According to the *Statistical Account of Dumfriesshire*, Langholm was elevated to a barony in 1610, and into a parish in 1703, becoming the seat of a Presbytery in 1743 by separating the five parishes of Eskdale from Middlebie and adding them to Castleton, which was formerly in the Presbytery of Jedburgh.

The first Parish Kirk of Langholm was built in 1703, with subsequent rebuildings in 1747 and 1779. The present Parish Church was built in 1845-46 on a new site.

According to the *Statistical Account of Scotland Vol XIII* the 1779 Church, the ruins of which still exist, was commodious – it could accommodate 800 sitters – but not elegant. It stood east from the town centre, on the side of a hill, which in winter rendered it not only cold but also when the frosts set in, of difficult access. According to *Langholm As It Was*, the accommodation in the Church was extremely primitive; for the most part the feet of the worshippers rested on the bare soil. People with means had boards laid down, whilst others provided themselves with plaited straw. Weeds of various kinds grew inside the Kirk. The gallery was approached by three stairways, all on the outside of the building. There was no vestibule, the door opening right into the building. This made the place draughty and cold. Whilst the congregation was assembling, the doors, even in winter, stood open.

The Church, rebuilt a second time in 1779-80, had barely been opened when trouble arose because the village of Langholm had greatly increased its population and the seating accommodation became a problem.

In due course, in 1845, the foundation stone of the present Parish Church was laid. It was built in the early Gothic Style on what was, without doubt, the finest site in the town, the Eldingholm, an easily accessible area of flat ground lying at the

Langholm Parish Church viewed from the suspension bridge in July 2004

junction of the Rivers Wauchope and Esk. The approach to the Church over the River Wauchope is by a private bridge. To the west, the Church is bounded by the Public Park which ensures that the site can never be built up.

The Church of Scotland and The United Free Church of Scotland joined in union in 1929. The Erskine Kirk became known as Langholm Erskine and the Parish Kirk became Langholm Old Parish Church. The last service in Langholm Erskine church was on 7th September 1975. In future, Church of Scotland Services would be in the Langholm Old Parish Church, to be known now as Langholm Parish Church.

As Langholm Erskine was linked with Westerkirk and Ewes, a further union of churches took place, the charge being renamed Langholm, Ewes and Westerkirk. Today Langholm Parish Church not only has regular services, but also is a focal point for several community events, including the Common Riding Service, musical performances at the Music and Arts Festival and school concerts.

The Catholic Faith in Eskdale

Until May 1960, there was no established Catholic Church in Langholm and Sunday Mass was occasionally held in the Eskdale Hotel.

In 1960 the Franciscan Sisters from Mullingar in the Republic of Ireland acquired Erkinholme from the Scott family and set up a Novitiate for young girls wishing to join the Order.

As time went by, it was found that fewer and fewer girls were entering the religious life and the Nuns then decided to convert Erkinholme into a home for the elderly, which they ran until 1995 when the enterprise became unviable.

During the Nuns' time at Erkinholme, there was a resident chaplain and Catholics were able to attend Mass at the private chapel. After Erkinholme was closed in 1995, Mass was held in the Day Centre.

In 1998 the parishioners, with the help of the Diocese, purchased the old South UF Church in Drove Road, which had been closed as a church in 1928, and over the years had been put to various uses. The Catholic parishioners initially refurbished and converted a small room underneath the building to a small chapel and this was utilised until such time as the refurbishment of the main building was completed.

St Francis Church in July 2004
formerly the South UF Church, or 'Toonfit Kirk'

In addition to being used regularly for Sunday worship, the church is also proving to be an ideal venue for concerts and the like.

Church buildings in Langholm

Following church closures and congregational amalgamations, only the two church buildings mentioned remain in use for regular worship. However, the buildings and traces of some non-parochial church buildings remain in the town.

Langholm Congregational Church was situated at the head of the Kirk Wynd and for a number of years, it was used by Edinburgh Woollen Mill as a store.

The Free Church, known as the Chalmers UF Church, was in Charles Street. After closure, in due course it became a cinema, then the local Scout Hall before being demolished and the site used for building flats, Charles Court.

The Erskine Church, "Toonheid Kirk" was the secession church and sadly remains both empty and without its weather-vane.

The Episcopal Chapel was a private chapel, belonging to His Grace the Duke of Buccleuch, and is situated in the grounds of Langholm Lodge. It was opened for worship on 9th September 1883 but now houses the Clan Armstrong Trust exhibition.

5

❧ Brigs, Stanes, Roads & Bars ❧

With the imminent birth of New Langholm, a bridge needed to be built across the Esk, which until then had been crossed at various fords – the main one being the Boatford at the point where the Wauchope joins this river. The Langholm Bridge was built in 1775 by Robert Hotson and was funded by public subscription. The original bridge, with its heavy stone parapet and narrow gauge roadway (which had a dangerously steep gradient at the New Town end), was extensively altered in 1880 at a cost of £1,188. The parapet walls were demolished and replaced on either side by flagged footpaths adding about ten feet to the width of the bridge. The west arch was also lowered by three feet, which greatly improved the gradient of the roadway on that side of the structure.

A mid-19th century sketch of Langholm from the Castle Hill

Dumfries and Galloway Regional Council widened and strengthened the bridge in 1995, to meet the demands placed on it by modern, heavy traffic. This need was forcibly brought home when a large hole appeared in the walkway in 1994, after a lorry had mounted the pavement. The work was carried out over a five-week period by Barr Ltd of Ayr, and at a total cost of approximately £400,000.

A bizarre incident happened on the bridge on 4th February 1824. It involved Simon Fletcher who, as his gravestone in the old Kirkyard testifies, was a Pensioner from the First Royal Dragoons and was present at Waterloo and 31 other battles. After leading such a dangerous and exciting life, he met a very ironic end when he died from the injuries he received after being attacked by a frenzied cow on the Langholm Brig! It seems that he had been walking leisurely across the bridge when the mad beast broke away from its owner, attacked him and ran him down. As he lay dying, the forty-five year old was said to have complained, in language more forcible than polite, of the indignity of being killed by a cow after having kept his feet throughout thirty-two battles!

As New Langholm became established, marked changes were made to the roads leading into and out of the town. The old coach road north ran down through land where the house of Clinthead stands today, before crossing the River Ewes at a ford behind the Toll Bar, at Ewes Foot. From there, it ran up the Chapel Path and through the farmlands of Bagra before meeting up with the present road just below Arkin.

The present road up the Ewes valley was constructed by Sir William Pulteney, the Laird of Westerhall in 1763, after obtaining permission through a special Act of Parliament. Up until then, this road was little more than a rough bridle path, and even the packhorses of the time found the route tortuous and difficult to follow. This fact is highlighted by a couple of entries taken from the Hawick Burgh records:

In 1661, "Robert Olipher, cordiner, was ordained to pay five pounds to the Bailies for disobeying them, by refusing to go and act as guide to the English troopers to Langholm". While in 1740, Thomas Sword was paid one shilling "for being a guide to the Langholm with an officer of the draugounes" (dragoons).

However, in 1822 a new road was cut through Walker's Hole and the Tourneyholm – a name referring to a spot where duels, or single combats took place – to a new bridge that had been built across the Ewes, near to the Whitshiels (or ocassionally Whiteshiels) Mill. This new bridge replaced an older bridge, which in 1772 was said to be "in utmost disrepair … and so narrow as not to permit passage of wheeled carriages". It was John Irving of Langholm Mill, the Right Worshipful Master of the local Lodge of Freemasons, who lowered the keystone of the new bridge into place, before declaring the same "well and truly placed".

The old road up Eskdale crossed the Ewes at the Ewes Foot ford before branching off in a north-west direction up the edge of the Castleholm. It forded the Esk at a place called Dowey's Pool Head, just below the Breckenwray, before heading up past Peden's View where it joined the present road through Eskdale. This old route became redundant when the new Eskdale road was built across the Meikleholm and up through the Galaside Wood. It was the existence of this new road, which spurred on the building of the Langholm Bridge.

The Bar Brae, that notorious hairpin bend cut into the end of the Bar Wood, was not built until 1886. Before that, the north end of Drove Road followed a very steep and dangerous course up past the Free Church Manse (now called Barbank). The new road was built as an approach to Erkinholme, the new residence of Mr Alex Scott, Manufacturer.

The old Wauchope road ran up behind the 'Mill En' at the top of Caroline Street and on past the head of Jamie's Brae to Scott's Knowe, which derived its name from John Scott (Scott the Piper), gamekeeper and Piper to the Duke of Buccleuch who lived there in the latter part of the nineteenth century. From here it ran along the loaning to the Becks Burn and past Ha' Crofts. It then continued along the hill below the Caulfield and met with the current road near Wauchope School House.

The present Wauchope road, which runs by way of the Pool Corner and Manse Brae, was built about the year 1794, and as a direct result of the Turnpike Road Act of 1751. This law allowed parish councils to set up turnpike roads where tolls were levied on all traffic which used them, apart from funeral processions. The money from these tolls was used to maintain and improve these roads. This scheme revolutionized transport and communication by converting what were little more than rough cart tracks into an efficient network of public highways.

There were three Toll Bars in Langholm, one on each of the turnpikes leading out of the town. The Townhead and Townfoot Bars still exist today as private houses, while the Wauchope Bar, a simple white-washed cottage in contrast to the other two bars, stood where the mill dam passes under the Wauchope road. The Wauchope Bar was demolished in 1937.

By all accounts, the carters who used these roads spent some riotous nights in the Toll Bars, which at one time were also licensed to sell liquor! It was not unheard of to see a queue of twenty to thirty horses and carts blocking the road outside while the drivers were inside sampling the 'Barley Brew'. Fiddleton Toll Bar, at the head of the Ewes Valley, was a particularly 'happy place' to be, especially on Thursday nights when the Langholm carters and Liddesdale lairds 'ca'd in' on their way home from the market at Hawick. The passing of the Roads and Bridges Act of 1878 brought about the end of the turnpikes, and the need for Toll Bars. The Langholm Bars had the distinction of being some of the very last to close down in Britain. On the last day of May 1883 the toll gates of Langholm, which had swung back and forth, summer and winter for well over a hundred years, were cleared away to give free access to and egress from the town in all directions. Few, if any, were sad to see the demise of the turnpikes, or suffered any pangs of regret when the toll-money jingled into the toll-man's bag for the last time.

A few hundred yards downstream from the Langholm Bridge lies Boatford Bridge or 'the Swing Brig' as it is known locally. As suspension bridges go it is unremarkable. However it has acquired a certain notoriety because of what happened to it just before its official opening in September 1871. The engineers and workers had arranged to have their photographs taken standing on the new structure. When the barriers were removed from each end, about sixty children and thirty grown-ups stampeded onto the bridge. No sooner had the local photographer, Mr Simon Carruthers, stuck his head under the cloth to take the photograph than disaster struck ... under this tremendous load the western suspension chain gave way, the bridge split in the middle and collapsed, albeit rather gently, into the river. It is said that in the panic that followed fully 200 people plunged into the Esk. One local myth had desperate mothers wading in and pulling bairns out as they floated past, and if they weren't theirs ... they flung them back in again! Within a few minutes, the news had reached all the factories in the town and nearly 2,000 people had descended on the disaster site. Luckily, the Esk was running low at the time and only two or three people were slightly injured. Mrs Elizabeth Donaldson aged 86, sustained the worst injuries – with two broken ribs. Had the river been in flood, as it so often was, the consequences might have been catastrophic.

The incident inspired one local poet, who wrote under the name 'Auld Brig', to pen the following lines: -

> 'E'er Telford's name was known to fame,
> Or Menai Straits were spanned,
> Across the Esk my arch was cast,
> And firmly still I stand.
>
> At length when trade had so increased,
> And people swelled the throng,
> Pedestrians wished to change their course
> Because the way was long.
>
> And over Esk, within my view
> A rival bridge was raised,
> And I, grown old, was slighted
> It, being new, was praised.
>
> But, woe betide its bolts and bars
> That were unsound or slim,
> And offered no security
> To precious life and limb.
>
> The Esk came not in roaring flood,
> The 'Souter Stane' stood bare–
> Nor thunder storm wi fury raged,
> Nor tempest filled the air.
>
> This Autumn sun shone bright at noon–
> No warning voice did tell–
> But ere its form was photographed,
> The trembling thing did fell.
>
> And old and young that stood there-on
> Kind providence did save,
> From what less fort'nate might have been
> To them a watery grave.

But when my rival's raised again,
As shortly it will be,
May it be worthy of this town,
Tom Telford's name, and me.'

The Twa Brigs
By 'Auld Brig'

The same contractors, Messrs A Hernauliwicz and Co, of London, sub-sequently rebuilt the bridge to an improved and strengthened design, and it was re-opened in a very unpretentious manner by the Bridge Committee in April 1873. The additional expense of £500 was raised by subscription and by a joint Art Union and Fire Engine Committee, which was engaged in raising funds to buy Langholm's first Fire Engine.

The bridge was damaged again in July 1904 during a massive flood, which rivalled the magnitude of the one which swept the Souter Stane away. At some point between ten and eleven o'clock at night on Friday 15th, a huge ash tree, carried downstream by the force of the river, collided with the walk-way of the bridge causing it to bulge out several feet, on one side. However, the damage was only superficial, consisting of a few broken rails and planks, and when the tree was cut away, the walk-way of the bridge recoiled back into its original position.

The Langholm Bridge and Souter Stane (on the far right) pre-1898

Before leaving the Esk, it is worth mentioning another local landmark that was situated at the river's edge where Grieve's Entry turns on to George Street, the large mass of greywacke known as 'The Souter Stane'. It was given this name because the Souters (shoemakers) and tanners of the town, such as John William and Thomas Brown and old Jamie Paisley, along with his two sons, Wattie and Andrew, would steep their hides in the river for a week to ten days at a time. To facilitate this they would attach them to the stone by using strong hair ropes that were tied to a metal ring sunk into its top. This stone was, from time immemorial, a gauge by which every known flood was measured. It finally succumbed to the power of the river during the massive flood of 1898, which was described by one witness as being "magnificent in its terrible grandeur", when the fury of the water broke up the stone and swept it away. The stone was held in such high esteem by the folk of the town that it is said that after it was washed away Robbie Anderson, the blacksmith whose smiddy was sited opposite in Elizabeth Street, sat down on his anvil and wept copiously at the loss of an 'auld freen.' The remaining portion of the Souter Stane was washed away by another massive flood in the 1930s.

6

❧ *A Backward Glance* ❧

Life in Langholm over 200 years ago

A fascinating glimpse of what life was like in Langholm some 230 years ago was given in a letter written to "The Town Baillie and others assembled at the Simmer or Lamb Fair and Common Riding at Langholm in 1843". The author, an 89 year-old native called Walter Miller, lived at Irthington near Brampton. For someone who had spent only three months at school and could barely write his name by the time he reached twenty, his memoirs of his early life in Langholm make fascinating reading.

He could well remember the cornfield that covered the land on which the New Town of Langholm was built: Charlie Little and his son, Christy, farmed this, while the Little Meikleholm, at the foot of the Galaside Wood, was farmed by John Heslop, who became a respectable carrier between Carlisle and Edinburgh. James Graham, a joiner from the country, built the first new house on this land and this was situated in the corner opposite Ewes Foot and Charlie's Pool. This treacherous pool, at the confluence of the Ewes and Esk, was said to have derived its name from a young man called Charlie Houndham (Hounam) who drowned there while bathing. The next pool downstream from this was the 'Dog Pool', under the east arch of the Langholm Bridge, where the townsfolk drowned dogs, cats and whelps, and anyone who could swim its length thought themselves "mighty fine swimmers". Mailie's Stream took its name from Mailie Huggon, a half-crazed woman who drowned there. It has been suggested that Mary's Stream, in the bed

The Mercat Cross as it stands today in the Library Gardens

37

of the Esk above the notorious local pool of Codgie, might be a corruption of this old place-name.

Miller could also remember the Tron, the strong oak post situated on the east side of 'The Cross'. The Mercat Cross stood in front of the grim old Tolbooth of Langholm, and was 'the platform' from which important proclamations were made; in later years the name came to mean that area of the Market Place rather than the cross itself. The Burgh weigh scales were hung from a cleek (hook) that was fixed to the top of the Tron and the country folk would bring their butter, cheese, tallow, raw hides, wool and skins to be weighed there on market or fair days. Here, according to Miller, all disputes over quantity or weight were ended, when justice was done by 'Tron Weight'.

There was not a single cart in the town of Langholm at that time, let alone a decent road it could travel on, apart from the High Street. Everything was transported in creels on horseback and that included all the peats, flax and turrs (turf cut for fuel), which were harvested on the hill. A type of simple sledge pulled behind a horse, called a Trail Carr, was used to gather in the crops of corn and hay. A man called Robin Beattie from Hawick brought the first cart that Miller could remember seeing … and it hardly deserved the name.

The most gruesome recollection he had was of the great heap of stones, which lay at the head of the Kilngreen. He had been told that it was here that witches were burnt. However, he was quick to add that these things happened long before his time! He recalled how their accusers, and the multitude, threw stones at these poor souls as they suffered unspeakable agonies in the flames. This claim is backed-up by *The Statistical Account for 1845*, which states that "several reputed witches were burnt in the last century, near to the old Castle of Langholm".

Local Witches, Bitches and Ghosts

The witches of Eskdale were so notorious and powerful that it is said that one local cleric fell so "forsaken of God, and wretched under their evil influence" that he committed suicide. It was said that they could cast their spell over the cow, to prevent her from yielding milk and over the churn, to hinder butter from being made. They were also said to possess the unique power of being able to transfer the pain of childbirth from the mother to the father!

During the seventeenth century, more than 4,500 men and women were burnt at the stake in Scotland, after being accused of Witchcraft, and some feel that this number is a serious under-estimation. This figure contrasts sharply with only 500 who were executed in England over the same period. Clearly, the English did not allow themselves to be overtaken by the frenzy that first gripped Scotland during the reign of James VI. Most accusations arose out of quarrels or disputes within small communities. Any woman who did not look normal, or act normally, was in danger of being branded 'a witch' by a malicious tongue, with all the terrifying consequences that followed. Those who practised the old pagan arts of folk medicine and healing could also arouse deep suspicion. A local myth has it that the Ewes Water never freezes over in winter because of the heat still eminating from the bodies of the burned witches.

One local woman who was branded a witch was Jenny Noble. It seems the only crime the poor woman ever committed was to hang herself in her own home, sometime during the eighteenth century. In those days the authorities would not allow suicides to be buried in consecrated ground, so her sons made a 'trail' of fir branches, put her body on it and dragged it to beyond the Common bounds, to the burngate. She was buried there, and since then this picturesque spot has been known locally as Jenny Noble's Gill. In a more gruesome version of this story, Jenny was dragged to this gill alive, and then hung from one of its trees, before being dragged through the neighbourhood.

Langholm also had a very singular way of dealing with scolding wives – a form of punishment known as 'The Branks' or 'Scold's Bridle'. This punishment, which was dealt out by the Chief Magistrate, was an iron bridle, which completely enclosed the head of the culprit, while a piece as sharp as a chisel, projected into her mouth to subdue her worst weapon … her vicious tongue! Once in place, the scolded husband would lead the harridan through the streets to be ridiculed by the townsfolk. The 1901 edition of *Chambers Dictionary* states that this punishment was still being used in Langholm in 1772. It has been claimed that this was much preferred to the ducking stool, which not only endangered the life of the culprit, but also allowed her to exercise her tongue by hurling abuse at onlookers, during those moments when her head was above water.

This corner of the Borderland abounds with tales of the supernatural. However, as John Mackay Wilson comments in his *Tales of the Borders*, "The march of intellect is gradually trampling under foot the legends, omens and superstitions which formerly flourished in their strength amid the wild fastnesses of the land; and they are seldom talked of now as things that have been, but never will be again."

The most celebrated local ghost story is that of The White Lady of Tarras. To the author's knowledge, this tale has never been told in any local book, and it is for this reason that he relates it to you now. John Wilson obtained it from an infirm old man, the son of this ghost-seer.

The tale is centred on Archie Brown, a poor weaver, and his wife Nance who lived in a cottage at Windy Hill, in the Tarras valley. Nance was a cheery, hardworking soul who faced the daily grind in a positive and forthright manner. However, Archie was far from happy with his lot in life and always grumbled that he had to work so hard for his bread when others, who were no better than himself, were "sittin' wi' their han's afore them, doin' naething ava".

Late one August night his fortunes changed in a most unexpected and sinister way. As Archie and Nance were preparing to go to bed after another day of toil, a soft rap came to the door of the cottage. Opening it, Archie was surprised to see a fine, but frail lady standing in the doorway. She explained in her genteel tongue, that she came from the south country and was heading towards Edinburgh to visit a friend, when she became lost. She asked if Archie might act as her guide to Langholm, but as it was late, they persuaded her to spend the night with them and continue her journey in the morning. After a supper of milk and bread, she lay down on their bed and fell into a deep and restful sleep. However, as she slept, Archie could not help noticing the silver buckles on her shoes and the fine gold rings on her delicate fingers, and dark and evil thoughts invaded his mind. The more he tried to sleep, the more these dark notions dominated his thoughts. In the end he raised himself on one elbow and lay staring at the frail creature in his bed, and thought what a happy man he would be if he had "a' her braw rings, the gowd (gold) that was in her purse, and her siller (silver) buckles and a'".

In the morning, after a hearty breakfast, the lady and Archie set off for Langholm.

As a token of thanks, she gave Nance a gold coin from her purse, which she very reluctantly accepted. All this time Archie stared intently at the bulging purse and sparkling coins in it.

Two hours later, as she busied herself about the house, Nance was startled by the approach of an unearthly wind, the like of which she had never heard before. It sounded like the groans of the dying, a desperate cry for help from the other side. Thinking that the roof was about to blow off the cottage, she ran outside, threw herself on the ground and covered her head with her apron. The storm got louder and louder, and yet Nance thought it strange that she could not feel the wind or see the grass swaying or the leaves rustling in the trees. Some neighbours saw Nance fall and rushed to help her back on to her feet. They were perplexed by her claims, for they had heard or felt nothing.

It was well into the gloaming before Archie finally came home. When Nance asked after the lady, Archie replied curtly, "She is safe at the end o' her journey".

When she went to put his coat back into the chest where it was kept, she noticed that it was spattered with fresh blood. This he explained away by saying that on his way home he had come across a man in Tarras who was trying to slaughter a massive sow. He had asked Archie to hold the beast as he butchered it, hence the blood on his coat. "Here's ane o' the bonny rings the leedy (lady) had on her finger in eer pocket! How cam ee by that?" enquired Nance. "Did I no tell ye afore, that the leddy was safe and sound at her journey's end? She wad insist on giein' me the ring, to keep for my kindness to her."

"Did she no send ony word back by ee?" asked Nance. "Ay," snapped Archie "She thanked ee for eer kindness, and said she'd send ye word when she got to the far end …"

Weeks and months went by and no news came of the lady. Archie went to Edinburgh and came back with pockets full of siller (silver coins), and a story of how an old friend had died, and left him the money. The lady was never heard of again, for she had neither kith nor kin to enquire after her.

There is reputed to be a stone on the bank of the Tarras with a mark on it, which all the storms and floods of the years have been unable to wash out. It is the mark of blood; and often the figure of a lady has been seen wandering in the mirk or in the bright moonlight near to it. A sober man may pass the Tarras a hundred times and see nothing, but after a Langholm hiring-day or Simmer Fair, when a man may have taken two or three nips o' the Barley Brew, he is almost certain to see The White Lady of Tarras.

7

Industrial Langholm

The Birth of Local Industry

The prosperity which Langholm has enjoyed over the past two centuries is due largely to the wool, cotton and linen industries. In 1791, the population of the parish was 2,540 and included six manufacturers of checks, threads and stockings, forty-three weavers, one tanner, two dyers, three bleachers, and a skinner. Dr Thomas Oliver, in his book *A Visit to Langholm and the History of its Manufactures*, states that this population was as large as that of Hawick and Galashiels put together. He, and several other authors have said this is why Langholm, the second largest town in Dumfriesshire at the time, was christened 'The Muckle Toon.' However, contemporary data on the populations of these towns contradicts this notion.

A century later in 1881, when Langholm reached its zenith in the industrial sense, the population of the parish had soared to 4,612. This explosion in numbers was partly due to a decrease in infant mortality rates brought about by better living conditions and the Victorian habit of producing large families.

The derelict Meikleholm Mill at the Mill En'
before 1891

By 1901 the population of the parish had fallen to 3,500, with 358 people living in the landward area and 3,142 living in the Burgh itself. There were 1,538 people living in the New Town and 1,604 in the Old Town. Today, with efficient forms of contraception available to all, the population of 'The Muckle Toon' is considerably less. The Census of 1991 quoted a civil parish population of 2,728, while the population of the town itself was 2,538. Ten years later, in 2001 the population of the town had fallen to 2,311.

The first census records for the Parish of Langholm which were compiled in 1841, list in detail, the trades and professions, which existed at that time.

There were: – 10 blacksmiths, 27 joiners, 5 clog makers, 25 shoemakers, 21 tailors, 30 masons, 4 gardeners, 4 nailors, 4 carters, 1 carrier, 3 distillers, 6 coopers, 3 skinners, 3 saddlers, 2 candle makers, 2 brewers, 2 tin smiths and 1 glazier, needle maker, broom maker, cutler, potter, tanner, tallow chandler, plasterer, maltster and a roadman.

In textiles and related industries there were: – 126 cotton and 14 woollen handloom weavers, 57 stocking makers, 9 wool carders, 5 wool spinners, 6 wool piecers, 4 wool slubbers, 7 cotton winders, 2 stocking sorters and 1 picker, stapler, scourer and a dyer's apprentice.

The first mention of a textile industry in the town dates from 1726, when Walter Macfarlane writing in *Geographical Collections Relating to Scotland* said, "within this year a wool combing trade is set up, what a pity it is, it wants a wool manufactory, being a great wool country."

Up until 1832, most of the manufacturers in the town were involved in the cotton trade. There were two mills at this time. One was the Meikleholm Mill, a cotton-spinning and weaving factory at the top of Wauchope Raw (Caroline Street), which later became Meikleholm Corn Mill, and was built in 1789 at a cost of £2,600. In 1794, John and James Carruthers, who owned the mill, were credited with making 20,000 yards of cotton checks and coarse linens. In its heyday in 1841, it had 3,552

Whiteshiels Mill

mule spindles in operation and employed about 90 people. After being converted into a corn mill, the building was finally demolished in 1891. It was the existence of this mill that led to the area being christened 'The Mill En'.

A vital adjunct to the trade was to be found at this same location, for McKnight's Dye House stood hard against the side of the Meikleholm Mill. Its founder, James McKnight, had the reputation as a splendid dyer of black, which was in great demand in those days when grey and shepherd's checks were in vogue. McKnight died in September 1907, the building having been demolished before this in 1902.

The other mill at this time was the Ewes or Whitshiels Mill, known to Langholm folk as the 'High Mill', and was built for Mr Irvine of Whitshiels Farm in 1797. This four-storey factory employed about 50 people who worked six days a week from 6 am to 8 pm with an hour's break for lunch. As Doctor Oliver comments in his book "luckily the workers didn't know anything better, or they would have reckoned the work slavery!" The fine cotton yarn, produced at the mill, was marketed in Carlisle and Glasgow to be used in the manufacture of superfine calicoes. At different times, this mill seems to have served as both a cotton and woollen spinning factory. This claim is backed-up by an entry in *Pigot's Directory of 1837*, which states that Thomas and Alexander Renwick, who were worsted spinners in the town, then owned it. The machinery was powered by a large 20 hp water wheel fed with water from the Ewes nearby, via a mill lade. The existing house on the east side of the bridge probably served as the mill office while the small field on the opposite side of the river, known as the 'Lint Dub', was where the lint was spread out to dry after being steeped in the river. After a somewhat chequered career, the mill was destroyed by a massive fire on 23rd December 1872. The blaze was discovered at 3 am by the night watchman at Messrs Bowman's Mill who noticed a telltale orange glow in the sky. By the time the fire brigade arrived, all floors were alight and part of the roof had collapsed. They wisely decided to concentrate their efforts on the adjoining buildings and were able to save the wool store, dye works, the scouring and drying house and the neighbouring workers' cottages. The damage done was estimated to be in the region of £4,000 – £5,000. The owners, Andrew Byers & Son, put the remaining buildings on the market, but were unable to find a buyer. The buildings were demolished soon after and the mill lade was filled in.

Fire was a constant threat to the mills owners. In 1870, it was commented, "it almost seems incredible that a town of the increasing importance of Langholm should be destitute of a fire engine". Consequently Langholm's first fire engine arrived in the town on 5th July the following year. This steam-powered vehicle, known as 'The Esk', was supplied by Messrs Merryweather & Son. It was bought by public subscription and was only the second of its kind in the whole of Scotland. On the evening of the day it arrived, 2,000 people watched it 'being put through its paces' as it extinguished a massive bonfire on the Kilngreen. The engine's furnace was lit on a signal given by Hugh Dobie, Acting Chief Magistrate, and within seven minutes steam was raised. River water was then pumped on to the flames, and within three minutes the fire was reduced to a pile of smouldering ashes! The following day the engine amazed onlookers at Waverley Mills by throwing a stream of water over the top of its tall chimney!

Langholm Distillery stood on a picturesque, rocky promontory three-quarters of a mile south of the town, wedged between the main road and the river Esk. It

'The Esk', Langholm's first fire engine

drew river water for cooling and power, but used the waters from the celebrated springs on Whita Hill to process its whisky. According to Alfred Barnard, author of *The Whisky Distilleries of the United Kingdom*, the Langholm Distillery was one of the oldest in Scotland, having been established in 1765. However, this claim does not tie in with local records. The *First Statistical Account for Dumfriesshire*, written in 1793, makes no mention of a distillery or a distiller in the list of trades in the town. Furthermore, the account goes on to say that "since this was written, Little & Co have erected buildings and machinery upon the River Esk for a paper manufactory", which suggests that this business pre-empted the distillery.

In addition, in his reminiscences, Simon Irving of Langholm Mill states "perhaps few now know that the Langholm Distillery was formerly a paper mill. When the buildings were sold my father became the purchaser, but soon resold them, and then after a time the buildings were adapted for a distillery."

The paper mill employed twenty workers who produced 80 reams of paper a week, with a total production valued at over £4,000 per year. The paper produced was made from cotton and linen fibre and not from wood fibre as it is today. The mill's large waterwheel supplied the energy required to pulverise the cotton and linen rags used in this process. By 1812, the paper mill had ceased production, with the premises being advertised for sale in the *Dumfries Weekly Journal* in April 1815.

John Arnott converted the buildings into a distillery in 1818 and ran the business until it went bankrupt in 1826. The company's debts totalled £4,850 and the main creditors were the Leith Banking Co and Connell & Co, bankers in Carlisle.

Langholm Distillery in the late 1800s

Other smaller creditors included the local cooper, a maltster and the local colliery, suggesting that too much of the firm's capital was tied up in bonded whisky.

James Kennedy and his partner John Connell, a member of the Carlisle banking family, revived the company again in 1832. Kennedy later went on to build the sister distillery of Glentarras, four miles south of Langholm in 1839. Under the Connell family's control, the Langholm distillery became famed for its malt whisky, which owed its fine quality to the peculiarly soft nature of the water from Whita Well. Matured in sherry wood, which gave it "a rich and silent flavour", the 'Old Small-Still Malt' sold particularly well in England as a 'self whisky' and was also used for blending elsewhere. The company produced a famous blend called 'Mountain Dew' and claimed to be the only known producers of the remarkably flavoured Birch Whisky, made using a secret recipe which had been handed down 'from father to son'. In the 1880s, 5 year-old malt whisky sold for 17/6d a gallon, while the same quantity of 10 year-old malt cost £1, carriage paid. The distillery, like the paper mill, was powered by a massive water wheel supplied with water from the River Esk through a channel cut into the solid rock. It had

LANGHOLM DISTILLERY

LANGHOLM, N.B.

PROPRIETORS:
ARTHUR CONNELL.
WILLIAM A. CONNELL.

Pure Malt Whisky Distillers.

Established 1765.

THE Proprietors of the above old-established Distillery beg to draw attention to their **Old Small-Still Malt Whisky**, which has long been much esteemed by connoisseurs who appreciate a mellow Liqueur Whisky.

This Whisky is not a blend, but a perfect self Whisky, made from Pure Malt only, of the very finest quality. The water used in the making is of a peculiarly soft nature, from the celebrated **Whita Well**, on the Eskdale Hills, and to the properties of this water, no doubt, is owing in a great measure the excellent quality of their Whisky. Messrs. Connell have a large Private Connection, and supply the above Whisky in 10-Gallon Casks and upwards at the following prices :—

5 years old	- 17/6 per gallon, carriage paid.		
Terms—Cash.	8 ,, ,, - 18/6	,,	,, ,,
10 ,, ,, - 20/-	,,	,, ,,

Messrs. Connell know the difficulty the public have in procuring a genuine Malt Whisky, suitable for private use, direct from a Distillery, but they have perfect confidence in recommending, as such, their **Old Malt Whisky**, matured in Sherry Wood, which they know will give entire satisfaction, and for which they solicit a trial.

SAMPLES ON APPLICATION.

An old advertisment for Langholm Whisky

an annual output of 46,000 gallons and stored 121,000 gallons of spirit in twenty different warehouses.

Arthur Connell, John's son, was an indomitable character. In 1852, he found himself in bitter dispute with the townsfolk over the Whita Well water rights. He claimed that the Distillery Company had a right to part of the water from this well. This incensed the townsfolk who, as tenants of the Ten Merklands of Langholm, claimed the God-given right to use the water from their 'ain hill'. Indeed two and a half years before this a committee had been set up and funds raised to pipe water to the town from the well, and the committee had gained the consent of the Duke of Buccleuch and other landowners to do this. However, the only drains which currently existed were to Langholm Distillery, and the Connell family fought hard to keep these channels open by bribing landowners, over whose ground they passed, with bottles of Langholm Whisky! The situation was made worse by the fact that a heavy drought had meant that most of the wells in the town were dry that year, while thousands of gallons of pure water from Whita Well were running to waste at the distillery.

The situation reached crisis point when Arthur Connell announced, at a meeting of the Water Committee, that no water from the well would be made available for this scheme for the town's inhabitants.

So for the second time the people 'rose up in defence o' thir property'. On the evening of Monday 26th April, a group of young men went out to the well and cut a rough drain down into the town, so channelling all the water down the Kirk Wynd and away from the Distillery. During the Grand Procession, which was organised to celebrate this victory, Pete Wheep (Peter Graham) the Town Drummer and Fair Crier sang the stirring 'Blue Bonnets over the Border' from the Miller's Hill. However, this jubilation was short lived, for, on the following Wednesday morning, a report quickly spread though the town that Mr Connell and a band of men were on their way to retake the well by force. A warning flag was hoisted at the well, and a drumbeat to arms was sounded as a large force of men, women and children rushed up the hill to confront the usurpers. In this instance the confrontation was relatively good-natured and Connell and his men left with the temporary drains still in place. However, at 10 pm that night the alarm bell on the Kirk rang out again to warn that Mr Connell had returned to take the site, with re-enforcements from Canonbie! The frenzied scene as hundreds rose from their beds and ran in panic to the well, which was by then enshrouded in an eerie mist, was said to be indescribable and unique in the annals of local history. Again no effort was made to retake the well and a guard was put in place in case of further attack. However, the next day summonses were issued to three leaders of the vigilantes for an alleged assault on John Connell. They were committed to trial but were released on bail. The Water Committee asked that the case should be decided by Sheriff Trotter, Sheriff Substitute for the county. However Mr Connell did not agree to this. In the end the Connell family relented and put forward a compromise, that the town should receive two-thirds of the water from Whita Well while the distillery would receive the other third. The townsfolk unanimously accepted this offer and as a gesture of goodwill on his part, John Connell paid one half of the costs of uniting the Whita and Donks streams at a cistern near to Whita Well.

Local folklore tells that a pious hermit once lived in a cell on the side of Whita, near the well. This holy man led such a blameless life that he was canonised during his lifetime and became known as Saint Thorwald (from the old Norse meaning Thor's power). It was claimed that he could produce a magical elixir, which had remarkable curative powers, and that travellers from far and near visited him to taste this healing liquor. After his death, a natural spring appeared near to where the hermit had lived. Perhaps this elixir was the original 'Mountain Dew', which he brewed in a crude still in his cell using the celebrated waters from Whita Hill.

The distillery was forced to close in 1917 due to a national shortage of barley and the failing health of the sole proprietor, Arthur Connell. Penfold's of Brampton demolished many of the buildings at the north end of the distillery in 1926. In 1927, the Tolson family from Ossett in Yorkshire bought the empty buildings. Two years later, they demolished the warehouses and built a bungalow on the site, while the buildings at the south end were converted into the Border Esk Filling Station and Garage. The only remnant of the distilling days John Tolson could find was an Excise man's dipstick!

Another fascinating relic of these bygone days had already been rescued from the business before it closed down – an illicit whisky still. Realising the potential it had, the local Excise Officer tried to render it useless by punching holes in it, but Robert Jeffrey, the local blacksmith and engineer, soon soldered these. He and another local worthy, Gordon Morrison, then fired it up on the kitchen stove in a brave attempt to brew up a batch of poteen! The smell of raw alcohol in the area round Brewery House was said to be overpowering. As the local Excise Office was just across the road, the Jeffrey boys, John and Andrew, were sent outside to burn any old rags or paper they could find in an effort to mask the smell. As the temptation to 'kindle it up again' would always remain, the still was sold to a publican up north for display purposes only – or so he said!

Pigot and Co's Directory of 1825-26 mentions a Brewery on Drove Street owned by Messrs Irving and Scott. One half of this 'Ale and Porter Brewery' was put up for sale by public roup (auction) in May of that year. (Porter is a dark-brown bitter brewed from charred or browned malt.) In addition to the main Brewery, the premises included Granaries, Kiln and Malting premises, a large two-storey dwelling house, two other houses and a barn, byre, stable and garden. The Brewery, which was situated on the Brewery Brae, behind Brewery House, was sold by the owner Walter Chalmers to John Connell of the Langholm Distillery Company in April 1858. In December 1863, the premises narrowly missed being destroyed when the roof caught fire. It seems the fire had started when a spark from a chimney had fallen on the roof at a point where a slate had been displaced, and soot had accumulated. However, assistance was quickly at hand and the flames were extinguished before much damage was done. The property remained in the hands of the Connell family until well into the next century but by 1887, the Brewers listed in *Wilson's Eskdale and Liddesdale Directory and Almanac* were W & J J Paterson.

In 1894, according to the *Valuation Role for the County of Dumfries*, Richard Johnstone and Sons were running the business. Soon afterwards, brewing stopped and the premises were rented out to a Blacksmith, John Telford.

The author has been able to find very few references to either the Distillery or Brewery in the pages of the *Eskdale and Liddesdale Advertiser*. Even the obituaries to John and Arthur Connell make no mention of them owning such businesses. He can only conclude that this complete lack of information was due to the influence exerted by the Langholm Total Abstinence Society, which was particularly strong at this time.

Also mentioned in *Pigot and Co's Directory* is a Tallow Chandlery (Candle Manufactory) owned by James Hope, at 18 Drove Road. In the days before electric or gas lighting, the candle makers did a brisk trade and James Hope's establishment was one of the largest in the town.

At one time, there was a Nailor's forge nearby, at the top of Wapping Lane. It was run by Andrew Johnstone who commenced his business in 1860 selling 'all kinds of nails at moderate prices'.

There was also a tobacco manufactory at the head of Wapping Lane. In March 1786, Excise Officers from Dumfries raided the properties of two tobacco manufacturers, James Robson and Thomas Hamilton. On inspecting Robson's premises, they found he had in his possession 1,018 lbs of leaf tobacco, 2,514 lbs of tobacco stalks, 545 lbs of roll and 134 lbs of snuff. They argued that on average, each hundredweight of unmanufactured tobacco should yield only 20 lbs of stalks, and as he possessed 2,514 lbs of stalks he must have handled much more tobacco than he was certified to do.

In Hamilton's house, they found 891 lbs of leaf, 633 lbs of stems (stalks), 504 lbs of shag (coarse, cut tobacco) and 483 lbs of rolled tobacco. This quantity fell within the limits set out by the certificates he owned but, on examination, these documents were found to be forgeries! Consequently, the tobacco from both houses was declared contraband and seized by the Officers. It was then loaded onto a cart and taken to Dumfries, where it was burned at the Cross.

Langholm also had a thriving hosiery and stocking industry, which started about the year 1790. By 1830, there were three hosiery factories in the New Town. Thomas Renwick's Mill was sited in the old buildings which were subsequently taken over by Messrs Reid & Taylor, and which had been partially built using stone taken from the auld Kirk on the hill. Andrew Byers' factory (built in 1858) lay off the west side of what is now Thomas Telford Road, while George Chambers' premises were beside the mill dam (lade) in or off Henry Street. The stockings made in these premises sold for between 2/6d and 6/- a pair and proved so popular that demand often outstripped availability.

The last stocking frame to be operated in the town belonged to Johnnie Beattie who lived in the cul-de-sac of cottages called Irving's Close, which was sited where the lodge to the Thomas Hope Hospital stands today.

Two main pioneers of the textile trade in Langholm were David Reid and Andrew Byers. They began by making shepherds' plaids or 'mauds' and shepherd check trousering, which they sold on foot to the towns within a circuit of thirty to forty miles.

At the outset, this involved only one or two handloom weavers. However, by 1845 there were 50 stocking makers and 260 weavers in the town, although this number would also include those involved in the cotton trade. Six years before this there were reckoned to be at least 100 handloom weavers in New Langholm alone. Many were crowded into 'back rows' in the area around Moodlawpoint where they struggled between their 'four posts of misery' (the treadle hand-loom) to eke out a living. There was a particularly famous nest of weavers between Henry Street and the mill-dam called 'The Crystal Palace' because of the amount of glass in the roof of the building. One handloom weaver interrogated by a commission said that he needed to work "dooble desperate" to make 2/6 a week. The standard of living became so bad that the Duke of Buccleuch was finally forced to intervene. In the fiscal year 1840-1, he provided £830 of relief for weaving families in the town.

However, even if money was in very short supply, enough could always be found for 'the bare essentials'. The story is told of the weaver who, when asked whether the piece he was working on would be finished that day, replied very cryptically, "If IT comes, it will not come; if IT does not come, it will come." The first IT referred to the greybeard of whisky, the second to the piece. Therefore, if the whisky arrived the piece would not get finished; if it did not arrive, it would get finished. With whisky at only 18d a quart, there was every chance it would arrive.

Apart from the 'boozy' few, the 'Knights of the Shuttle' were intelligent, articulate men who took a keen interest in the affairs of the day. In one particular 'nest' in John Glendinning's weaving shop, which was sited behind the Town Hall (and later became Telford's Joiner's business), they had a good library and their own debating and literary society. This spot, at the foot of Jouker's Close, was the meeting place for the leading politicians of the town. They would gather there on summer nights and discuss affairs of state from a severely radical standpoint, and in time the area became known as 'Parliament Square'.

The Langholm Railway – Leave the world and enter Langholm!

The effects of the Industrial Revolution were being felt throughout Britain: not least was the introduction of the railways into areas which had, like Langholm, been relatively isolated at the start of the nineteenth century. But a railway linking Langholm to the outside world was complicated by the machinations of rival railway companies, and the presence of coal at Plashetts, in the North Tyne valley, and at Canonbie.

The Hawick branch of the North British Railway was opened on 1st November 1849. However, it was to be a further thirteen years before the Waverley Route from Edinburgh was completed between Hawick and Carlisle.

In 1845, the North British Railway obtained powers to build the Hawick branch and in the following session they applied to Parliament for further powers to extend the line through Langholm to Carlisle. The Caledonian Railway opposed this extension, and in due course the North British Company's plans were thrown out by the Government Committee. Matters dragged slowly on, with meetings in Hawick of many of the manufacturers who felt the need for a railway to the south, but no substantial progress was made until 1856 when a survey was made of the Liddesdale route. The Caledonian Railway also had plans for a station in the Lower Haugh in Hawick with a railway through Teviotdale and Langholm to Carlisle. (Over 1,500 women who used the Lower Haugh as a washing green objected to this scheme.)

To the astonishment of many inhabitants, the claims of the Caledonian Railway Company's Langholm line were approved and those of the North British Railway's Liddesdale scheme rejected. So indignant were the supporters of the Liddesdale railway, that a meeting outside the Town Hall in Hawick attracted some sixteen hundred people expressing the view that the decision was totally against the wishes of the people of the south of Scotland. An appeal was taken to the House of Lords which resulted in the Langholm Bill being thrown out.

In 1859 the railway battle raged again before Parliament and on Tuesday, 22nd March, it was announced that the Liddesdale scheme had triumphed. One factor had been the inferior quality of the coal at Canonbie compared with that of the North Tyne coal from Plashetts.

Langholm had come close to having a through line to Hawick, worked by the Caledonian Railway Company, who would have built another station in Hawick away from the existing North British one.

In many ways, Langholmites felt cheated. However, with the benefit of hindsight, perhaps a Caledonian Railway branch through Langholm to Hawick would not have served the town as well as inhabitants would have wished. Kelso had a station shared by the North British and the North Eastern, who although nominally friendly railway companies, did not always run trains with through connections from St Boswells to Berwick. Both the Caledonian and North British Railway companies (who were arch rivals) had separate stations in Peebles but little effort was made to allow traffic to interconnect between the stations. Perhaps Langholm people would have experienced great difficulty in making a day trip to Edinburgh via Hawick. They might have found themselves, and the goods manufactured in the town, routed to the south to Carlisle by the Caledonian Railway and then north by that company's main line via Beattock to Edinburgh – with all the revenue going to the Caledonian Railway. Via Hawick, of course, the revenue would have been shared with the North British Railway Company.

Thus Langholm, its inhabitants, and its blossoming industries, had to be content with a seven-mile single-track branch line, although a main-line, with direct connections to the north and south, worked by one railway company from Edinburgh to Carlisle would have been the ideal situation.

However, as a consolation to the people of Langholm, the train fare north of the town to Hawick and beyond was calculated as if the branch line ran directly north and not south to Riddings before going north again. This led to the strange situation that the fare from Langholm to Edinburgh was cheaper than the fare from Canonbie to the capital, although Canonbie was some six railway miles shorter.

The last mail coach from Hawick ran on Monday, 30th June 1862, via Langholm to Canonbie and the main line from Carlisle to Edinburgh was opened to regular traffic the following day.

The first train arrived in Langholm on Tuesday, 29th March 1864, carrying the turntable to be installed in the yard. The line was officially inspected the following Monday. The local paper records that passenger and goods traffic started on Monday, 11th April.

Less than a month had gone since the opening of the Langholm branch line, before apprehension was expressed by a number of "self-elected inspectors" at the state of Byreburn viaduct (where one of the piers went as far below the surface of the burn as it was above). Subsidence caused by a slippage into the old coal workings had resulted in the collapse of a portion of the crown of the third arch from the Canonbie end of the viaduct. Trains were halted at each side of the viaduct, and passengers had to walk across the unsafe portion! In early May 1864 the Langholm to Canonbie train service was temporarily discontinued and the omnibus reinstated.

Feelings ran high in the town. It was felt that, having obtained the monopoly of train services, the North British Railway Company was being tardy in its efforts to resume the service. H Dobie, the acting Chief Magistrate, stated that the line should have been kept open as it had been in the week following the slippage. It was resolved that a statement would be laid before the railway directors and if necessary, the whole matter would be brought before the Board of Trade

In due course the railway re-opened on Monday, 2nd November 1864, with six passenger trains running on weekdays and two on Sundays.

A letter in the *Eskdale and Liddesdale Advertiser* in December complained about the "unholy" Sabbath trains. The Sunday trains were discontinued in February 1865, the reason being given that they did not pay. The local paper commented that "The Sabbath rest will be a great boon to the employees along the branch, who, we understand, outnumber the passengers travelling from Langholm on the Sabbath-day." No more Sunday trains ran in the next hundred years, except the occasional excursion. Ironically, the very last passenger train, an enthusiasts' special from Glasgow, ran on Sunday, 29th March 1867, almost three years after the line had been closed to regular passenger traffic.

Table 176		CARLISLE, RIDDINGS, and LANGHOLM			

Miles		Week Days only						Miles			Week Days only					
		mn	mrn aft	aft E b	aft S b	aft b	aft b				mn mrn mrn		aft E b	aft S b	aft b	aft b
—	Carlisle...........dep	9 20	1 23 1 33	4 49	8 15			—	Langholm...........dep	712 9	6 1054	..	1 23	1 25 3 20	6 24	9 32
9¼	Longtown................	9 43	1 46 1 54	5 13	8 43			4½	Gilnockie A.............	724 9	9 11 6	..	1 29	1 43 3 29	6 35	9 42
11½	Scotch Dyke...........	9 49	1 52 1 59	5 18	8 49			7½	Canonbie................	730 9	14 1111	..	1 34	1 39 3 34	6 38	9 48
14	Riddings............arr	9 54	1 57 2 35	22	8 53			9½	Riddings............arr	734 9	18 1115	..	1 38	1 43 3 38	6 42	9 53
—	167 Edinburgh(Wav.dep	..	6 20 ..	10 5	2 30	5R55		9½	167 Edinburgh(Wav.arr	..	1226 ..		4 49	4 49 7 13	9R58	...
—	Riddings...........dep	747 9	55 1 58	2 45	26	8 54		—	Riddings............dep	746 9	54 1116	..	1 39	1 44 3 39	6 47	9 54
15¼	Canonbie............	752	10 02 3 2	9 5	31	8 59		9¼	Scotch Dyke............	752 9	59 1121	..	1 44	1 49 3 45	6 52	10S0
16¾	Gilnockie A...........	757	10 5 2 8 2	14 5	37	9 6		11¾	Longtown	758	10 5 112c	..	1 5c	1 58 3 52	7 1	10 6
21¼	Langholm.......... arr	8 6	1015 2 18	2 23	5 46	9 16		21¼	Carlisle............arr	815	1022 1148	..	2 13	2 18 4 14	7 28	1 27

A Station for Claygate.   **b** Thro Trains between Carlisle and Langholm.   **E** or **E** Except Saturdays.
R Via Longtown.   **S** or **S** Saturdays only.
For **OTHER TRAINS** between Carlisle and Riddings, see Table 167.

An extract from a 1946 Bradshaw railway timetable.
The Summer Fair night train would have arrived at 9.16 pm

The branch line and the successive railway companies, the North British, the London and North Eastern Railway and finally British Railways served the town well during times of peace and times of strife.

Everyday traffic included textiles, coal, newspapers, post, whisky (until the distillery closed), general merchandise and parcels.

A scene from the last day of the passenger service, 13th June 1964

Unusual traffic included specials to the new munitions factory at Gretna during WWI and, in WWII, double headed trains drawing tanks to and from the Camp on the Castleholm. On occasions the Cornet's horse came by rail.

In the early days the station at Langholm had an overall roof, an engine shed (the remains of which can be seen in the photograph opposite) and a turntable for the branch locomotive, often "Langholm" or "Gretna". After the engine shed closed, single-coach steam rail-cars, usually "Nettle" or "Protector" were introduced on some services between the wars.

A British Railways sign – and a gas lamp

Excursion traffic was a feature of the branch line. There were many Rugby Specials run to Murrayfield and Sunday School trips to Silloth. But excursion traffic was not always out of Langholm. The town had, especially at the turn of the nineteenth century, "mill outings" from south of the border. The local paper records a number of occasions when upwards of some 400 visitors descended on the town.

However, after WWII, private transport increased and in common with rural branches all over Britain the number of passengers using the Langholm branch decreased to the extent that the passenger service became uneconomic.

When the Beeching plans were announced in 1962, the Langholm Branch and the Waverley Route were proposed for closure. A public meeting was held in the Buccleuch Hall in Langholm on 18th October 1963, when representatives of Langholm Town Council and other objectors were able to put forward their cases of hardship to members of the Transport Users' Consultative Committee. Both oral and written objections were considered by the Committee, their unanimous conclusion being that, although the closure of the Langholm Branch would be inconvenient to some, and might even be a hardship to a few, the closure of the branch would go ahead.

The Beeching Axe, which meant that the sound of a train would never be heard again in many rural valleys, fell in Eskdale on 15th June 1964, the last passenger train leaving Langholm on Saturday 13th June.

The layout at Langholm station which would serve only freight traffic in future was simplified with the removal of the track beside the platform. The freight service lasted until 17th September 1967. Soon afterwards the lines were lifted and the Railway to Langholm became just a memory.

Of course, had the North British Railway been able to construct a through line via Langholm to Edinburgh as had been planned in 1845, then the situation would have been much different: Langholm would have been on a through main line. One might even speculate that this route might just have survived the Beeching cuts long enough, as did the Settle and Carlisle line, to be in existence today, bringing trade and tourists to the town.

Almost all that remains in the town, at Townfoot, is a cairn on the site of the station. But where else in the world would a Flute Band arrive at a railway station, which doesn't exist, to meet exiles – passengers on a train which hasn't run since the early 1950s, and parade them back to the town?

The signalman at Riddings Junction probably was right when he used the phrase "Leave the world and enter Langholm" to a family moving into the town!

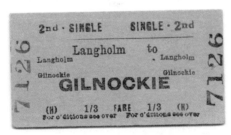

8

🍀 *The Local Tweed Barons* 🍀

In the space of a few short months at the beginning of 1874, Langholm lost no fewer than seven of its most prominent and influential figures. These men, through their enterprise and ability, had elevated Langholm from yet another small town, which was seldom heard of beyond the confines of its own hills, to a nationally renowned centre of excellence for the production of textiles. The image which the town has as an independent, resourceful and proud community, is due in no small way to their insight and effort. It was said at the time, "We cannot all attain to leading positions, but we can all cultivate and practise those excellences of character which are the only safeguard of our commercial mortality and the hope of our country".

Reid & Taylor's factory before the devastating fire of 1933

The foundations to one famous local business were laid in 1839 when David Reid's son, Alexander, a handloom weaver, saw potential in buying lengths of cloth from other local weavers and marketing them in Carlisle. In 1848, he met and went into partnership with a draper from Brampton, called Joseph Taylor. Mr Taylor and his partner, Mr Gardhouse owned a branch shop in Langholm High Street where they sold clothes. This venture with Mr Reid proved so successful that they were able to offer employment to 120 handloom weavers throughout the town. From these humble beginnings grew one of the most prestigious companies in the whole of the Scottish Borders – Reid & Taylor of Langholm. In 1851, they bought Alex Renwick's Cotton Mill on the corner of William Street and Elizabeth Street and extended and altered the building in stages, until by 1878 it was six storeys high (including an attic and basement) and was 106ft long and 60ft wide. On the front elevation a clock tower and spire rose to a height of 90ft, while above the staircase was a handsome octagonal belfry with pagoda roof. The clock tower housed a massive dead-beat motion clock with four illuminated opal glass dials. This massive building, with a total floor area of 36,000 square feet, housed 8 sets and 75 power looms, and gave employment to 400 people.

The company's most renowned product, 'The Twist Cheviot Suiting' won a gold medal at the Great Exhibition of 1851 and another at the South Kensington Exhibition of 1862.

Alex Reid's pioneering spirit led him to travel throughout Europe and Russia, where he marketed his cloths. In September 1871, Mr Reid held a massive picnic for workers and their families on a plot of land he had recently acquired north of the town. In total 600 people attended the event and the processions to and from it were accompanied by colourful banners and bands. Three years later, in 1874, tradesmen began to build a mansion called Craigcleuch on this site where, it was hoped, Mr Reid would spend the evening of a busy life. Dr Oliver claimed that the cost of building this house was in excess of £36,000. However some consider this figure excessive when compared with the cost of building other large contemporary stone buildings. Sadly, Alex Reid did not live to enjoy his beautiful home with its majestic views, for he died on 20th March 1874 before it was completed. General Sir John Ewart KCB, a gallant veteran of Crimean and Indian Mutiny fame, and the great grandfather of Lord Monro of Westerkirk and Langholm, subsequently bought the mansion.

Earlier, Mr Taylor had leased the farmhouse of Potholm from the Buccleuch Estates in 1867 and converted it into a pleasant residence with extensive gardens and vineries. Being a rather private gentleman, he could be seen driving his carriage and pair down the Langfauld Wood and through the grounds of Langholm Lodge on his way to the mill each day, avoiding the more public Eskdale road.

After Mr Reid's death the company passed into the hands of the local Graham family, and its fortunes waxed and waned, especially during the depression of the early twentieth century. In 1933, Fred Graham of Holmwood appointed Robert Richard Scott-Hay as a designer/manager. But within months of his arrival disaster struck when a massive fire destroyed the main factory building. D Stott, foreman baker at the Co-op, discovered the fire shortly before 4 am on the Monday after the Common Riding. It had started in the older part of the factory and for a while it was hoped that fire doors would prevent it spreading into the newer six-storey portion. However, this was not to be, for the flames leapt up into the second top flat, which was empty at the time, and it was not long before the entire structure was ablaze. At its height the flames were 90ft high and the terrific heat generated could be felt on the other side of the river on George Street. Flaming debris was carried a considerable distance by the wind; in fact burning wool and yarn were found as far away as Erkinholme. The only thing that prevented neighbouring buildings from being set alight was the fact that it was raining quite heavily, keeping all surfaces wet. At one point it looked as though the fire might spread to the neighbouring Tannery and the property owned by Mr & Mrs Sharp. They, like residents of William Street, took the precaution of removing furniture and leaving their homes. Fortunately the only damage to these buildings was some cracked windows and blistered paintwork! Langholm Fire Brigade needed the assistance of crews from Hawick, Carlisle and Dumfries before finally getting the fire under control.

Some said that the fire was started deliberately, although the management vigorously denied this. It was also said that one had been lit some weeks earlier, but had been spotted by a worker and extinguished. Another 'myth' which grew up round the event had one member of the Fire Brigade 'ower the bed, wi' his boots on' long before the alarm was raised! Local folk were so used to regulating their lives by the factory clock that for months afterwards they would automatically gaze upwards into thin air to see the time.

The stress caused by the fire, coupled with an existing long-term illness, led to the early death of Mr Graham in November 1933. The relatively inexperienced Mr Scott-Hay then faced the daunting task of building up the business again from the ashes of this disaster. Thanks to his incredible flair for marketing and advertising, he lifted the company to hitherto unseen heights of achievement. His policy of restricting his customer list to around fifteen accounts throughout the world, and then providing this 'chosen few' with the highest level of personal service, was the corner stone to his success. His motto, which he adhered to rigidly, was "quality is my hobby". He maintained that he always "sold up to a standard – and not down to a price" and was able to make a positive virtue out of the promotional phrase "The World's Most Expensive Double Twist Suiting". His natural flamboyance and flair for life made him, and the company, the best-known names in the Scottish Tweed trade. Scott-Hay invented the firm's famous logo, 'Rupert the Aristocratic Ram' in the 1950s, and it became a familiar emblem in high-class tailors' shops throughout America, Canada, Hong Kong and Japan. Although the world was his oyster, he would think nothing of driving miles in the dark to give illustrated lectures in small village halls in which he would extol the Reid & Taylor name. In April 1962 he achieved his life's ambition

R R Scott-Hay

when Sir William McTaggart, President of the Royal Scottish Academy, opened an art gallery which Scott-Hay had constructed on the mill site. This gallery, which is now named after Scott-Hay, was built with the sole purpose of bringing an appreciation of the arts to all members of his staff.

Mr Scott-Hay attended a mill party in the town in December 1965 but left early, as he felt unwell. Bedecked in his trademark fedora, black cloak and monocle, he bid adieu to his colleagues and the company, with a flamboyant swirl of his cloak. That theatrical gesture was a fitting farewell to this most colourful of characters, for Robbie Scott-Hay suffered a seizure at his home at Eskbank, Canonbie later that night and died the next day.

John A Packer became Managing Director of the firm after Scott-Hay's death and carried on the company's promotional traditions with a string of lavish events throughout the world. In one of his early extravaganzas he struck a novel note by flying a Norman Hartnell-designed Reid & Taylor collection around the principal capitals of Europe, launching a cat-walk show down the aircraft steps wherever it landed. In 1971, the company was honoured with the Queen's Award for Industry for Export Achievement. The company became part of the Allied Textile Group in 1965, and in September 1998 it was bought by the Indian textile company of S Kumars Nationwide Ltd.

Today Reid & Taylor (or 'the Factory' as it is known locally) supplies some of the leading names in luxury fashion including Chanel, Prada, Burberry and Givenchy, as well as the master tailors of Saville Row, and still has the reputation of being "The Makers of the World's Most Luxurious Cloths".

In 1852, there were at least eleven manufacturers in Langholm. Most of these mills had chequered careers and have long since been forgotten.

One such mill was the large, imposing Wauchope Mill (also known as Bowman's or McLaurin's Mill), which stood where the modern housing scheme, known locally as 'The Crudens', stands today. James Bowman, the founder, had started out in the dyeing and linen thread-making trades. In 1859, he moved into cloths, when the first stage of Wauchope Mill was completed. In 1866-67, a large extension was added. This three storey building, measuring 100ft by 50ft, was built to accommodate the spinning department. Unfortunately, a fire caused by the spontaneous combustion of damp wool destroyed the finishing department and one hundred pieces of cloth in 1868.

Two serious accidents occurred at the mill, highlighting how dangerous mill work was at that time. In October 1872 a fourteen year-old boy called Richard Kerr lost his arm after it was accidentally drawn into a carding machine. The limb was so badly lacerated that Doctors Carlyle and Stewart were forced to amputate. In June 1895, colleagues found Andrew Thompson, a mill worker from the Factory Entry, lying unconscious in a pool of blood next to some machinery. It transpired that while he had been cleaning the machine, a belt had caught his arm and he had been thrown violently to the ground, turning a complete somersault, before splitting his ear open on the side of the machine.

Wauchope Mill was taken over by Peter McLaurin in 1873, but suffered mixed fortunes before being destroyed in a massive fire in November 1896. The tall mill chimney stood 'sentinel like' in the midst of the ruin for another six years until it was razed to the ground by the local mason, James Elliot, in 1902. In *Lang Syne in Eskdale*, David J Beattie recounts how, after a violent storm in 1856, the

A group of weavers and tuners from Wauchope Mill

partially-built chimney suddenly developed a dangerous tilt of nine inches from the perpendicular. Thanks to the ingenuity of Willie Irving, a local builder, this was corrected by cutting a wedge-shaped section out of the freestone base on the opposite side from the tilt. Iron wedges supported the brickwork above and when these were slowly removed, the structure righted itself completely. The only remnant of this mill which exists today is the house known as Wauchope Cottage, which served as the mill office and which escaped the fire. But much of the fabric of Wauchope Mill still exists, for rubble from it was used as foundation for the Dam Side, that roadway between Henry Street and Eskdaill Street, which turned into a veritable 'sie o' glaur' during wet weather.

There was also a large dye works tucked in between Wauchope Mill and Eskdaill Street, which was run by Andrew Butler. The dye works survived the fire of 1896, but was forced to close down soon afterwards due to a lack of orders as this same fire had destroyed their best customer, Wauchope Mill.

Another prominent mill was Lightbody's Eskdale Mill. Thomas Lightbody had begun in business by selling the cloths made by various local manufacturers, and up until 1850 was credited with being able to carry his entire stock on his back. In his early years his spirit of adventure had led him to America, where he gained experience of life through his travels to its major cities. In 1860 he built a two-storey warehouse on the waterside south of West Street, and six years later an adjoining single-storey mill. The mill, which was approximately 80ft long by 60ft wide, had a row of cottages on the riverside that housed the main mill structure. On Mr Lightbody's death in June 1896, the business passed to his only son, David Lightbody, and when he died in 1916, his two sons, Thomas and Arthur, took the helm.

In *Oor Ain Folk*, David J Beattie claims that it was Thomas Lightbody senior who invented the word 'Tweed', the name now given to the world famous Border woollen cloth. He explains that Lightbody had sent a bunch of twill patterns to a well-known London merchant. In the covering letter he described the patterns as 'tweels', the local pronunciation for twills. Unfortunately his handwriting was rather poor and the recipient read the word as 'tweeds', and described it thus in the order which he sent back. Dr Oliver however, contradicts this, claiming that it was a Hawick man, James Hunter working for Wm Watson & Sons, who deserves the credit, and argues that Lightbody's Mill was not in existence when the word was invented.

When Lightbody's Mill failed in 1927 all the machinery was sold and Arthur Bell & Sons bought three of the Dobcross looms. The buildings were bought by a local farmer, J J Paterson of Terrona, and parts were used at various times as an Agricultural Society Store (The Farmers' Store), house, practice hall for Langholm Town Band, council waste paper store, timber merchants (G Ireland), and engineering workshops (Roy Taylor and latterly R A Russell & Co). In 1987, The Edinburgh Woollen Mill Ltd bought part of the building as a store, but this was later demolished to make way for new housing.

In 1848, a Hawick man, Walter Scott, started as a skinner treating fallen skins in premises in Albert Place (on the site where the Fire Station stands today) using the sum of £150, which he had borrowed from a friend. A short time later the company moved to their current premises in Elizabeth Street, near the Suspension Bridge. In 1870, he took out a lease on Holmfoot, at the south end of the town. He became renowned for his generosity, especially towards the Langholm Congregational Church, which was originally known as the Evangelical Union (EU) or Morisonian Kirk. Indeed before this kirk was opened in the Kirk Wynd, its followers worshipped in a make-shift chapel on the south side of Buccleuch Square, which had been converted from the 'bark-house' belonging to Mr Scott's tannery business. A bark-house was a building in which tree bark, a key component in the tanning process, was stored and processed. Mr Scott was a founder and generous supporter of this movement in Langholm and for that reason was given the honour of laying the foundation stone of this church in the summer of 1870. It was built on the site of The Ewe and Lamb, a notorious hostelry frequented by the drovers who used the Drove Road. It was claimed that many flocks of sheep spent an uncomfortable night lying on the Kirk Wynd while their drovers drank the 'wee small hours away' in this local hostelry.

Mr Scott's natural generosity was often open to abuse and it was said that all the 'leeches' that lived on charity knew exactly how much they could make out of him!

In time his nephew, Charles Paisley joined him as a worker and was paid the princely sum of £1 a week. He was reputed to be the highest paid worker in Langholm. In about 1890, Charles was promoted from manager to a junior partner, and after his uncle's death in 1899, took the business over as Charles Paisley and Sons.

Walter Scott was laid to rest in the ancient burial ground of Staplegordon, where the inscription on his gravestone bears testament to his great benevolence.

> *WALTER SCOTT, Holmfoot, died 20th January 1899 in his 80th year.*
> *A man of high Christian principles, respected and loved by all who knew him.*

Memorial tablets to both Walter Scott and his nephew Charles Paisley can be found in the east porch of Langholm Parish Church.

The company of Charles Paisley and Sons is now owned by Pittards plc but Robert Paisley, the founder's great grandson, still manages it along with his sons, Charles and Andrew. At most, it has handled 1.5 million skins per year and currently employs about sixty workers.

In 1866, William Little, who ran a drapery in the High Street, sold the drapery and started up a handloom manufacturing business on the east bank of the Esk at the Boat Ford. Two years later he went into partnership with William Anderson, a handloom manufacturer from the New Town, and built a two-storey building with attic, which is still standing. In 1869, Thomas Moses took over the premises as a woollen mill and called it the Ford Mill. He enlarged it by building shed extensions using £3000, which he had borrowed from Peter McLaurin, the London agent. By 1874 the company had failed and soon afterwards Moses joined Reid & Taylor as a designer-manager.

After passing through the hands of two other owners, the Ford Mill was finally bought by MacIntyre and Cairns in 1889. MacIntyre left the company after a short time and John Cairns was joined in the business by his father and brother, James.

The firm became famous as makers of beautiful Cheviot woollen grey cloths and fashionable woollen costume fabrics. Provost John Cairns died in 1938 and the mill, then known as Cairns of Langholm Ltd, ceased production during the difficult times which preceded WWII. One of the main factors that brought about this closure was a bad deal to produce cloth for overcoats for Russian servicemen.

In 1940, the mill was sold to the Admiralty for a Strategic Stock Pile store.

In 1949, Jack Armitage, a mill owner from Blackburn in Lancashire, bought the premises for £10,000 from the owner, John Maude. Mr Armitage owned a mill called the Woolly Mill, which specialised in producing cloths with cotton warps and woollen wefts and he and his son, Edwin, brought this expertise to Langholm. Jack also introduced the first automatic bobbin-changing looms to the town. For the first ten years, the mill only carried out the weaving of traditional cloths, but in 1959 a finishing plant was incorporated into the existing buildings. Among the more unusual requests they received was to supply the monks at the nearby Monastery of Samye Ling with the maroon material used in their traditional robes. An especially fine piece of material had to be woven for the impending visit of the Dalai Lama. Latterly the company diversified into producing cloth for worsted ties and then went into scarf weaving for the famous scarf company, Sammy. In September 1991 the company was forced to close.

In that same year, Illingworth Morris bought the premises and moved the world famous name of J & J Crombie of Aberdeen down to Langholm. The state of the art machinery they installed was to make the Ford Mill the finishing plant for the entire Crombie product, and also for the sports jacketing then being woven at the sister plant of R G Neill & Son. It was a blow to the economy of the town when this grand old mill closed its gates for the last time in July 1998.

A notable dynasty of mill owners were the Scotts of Waverley Mills. James Scott was a general merchant in Newcastleton and Claygate, Canonbie, where he dealt in groceries, iron, slates, oil, gunpowder, seeds etc. Much of his prosperity came from his dealings with the workmen who were employed in building the railway from Hawick to Carlisle, and the branch line into Langholm. This very enterprising man also blended his own whisky to sell in England and had a retail and wholesale business selling textiles.

James Scott of Claygate,
co-founder of Waverley Mills

In 1864 his son, Alex travelled to Langholm on the new steam train to start work as an apprentice at Reid & Taylor. He soon left 'the Factory' and started up on his own with a few handlooms in a building on the corner of Henry Street and Walter Street, which had been erected by a handloom manufacturer called Hyslop, and was known as 'Overlength Hall'. Due to the success of this venture, he was able to persuade his father to join him as a partner in 1865 and to put up half the money towards the building of Waverley Mills. However, James Scott insisted that his eldest son, John should also be a partner in this new company to act as a restraining influence over Alex, whom he thought to be impetuous and rather inexperienced.

The building of Waverley Mills began in 1866 at an initial cost of £3,600. A year later, in February 1867, guests were invited to a massive ball and opening supper to launch the new business of James Scott and Sons. The supper, for workers and tradesmen involved in the construction, was held in the large hall of the Eskdale Temperance Hotel, and was set out in "Mr Franklin, the proprietor's best style." The Grand Ball, attended by four hundred "fair women and brave men," was held in the third flat of the new mill. Numerous songs were sung throughout the evening, and the future prosperity of the firm was toasted by one of the contractors. It was not until "the morning bells pealed out their merry chime" that the company finally broke up.

Four years later a large extension was added to the existing building and from that time the company maintained a high reputation in the tweed trade. Unlike other small Scottish firms, James Scott and Sons did not rely on agents, like Peter McLaurin, to sell their cloths for them. Alex Scott was a very astute businessman and first-rate traveller, and he and his friend James Sanderson (from Galashiels) effectively removed the middleman by selling directly to the high-class merchants of London. It was this shrewd approach to business which proved to be the key to their success.

The two brothers built fine houses in the town to reflect their prosperity.

Alex Scott built Erkinholme, which he and his family first occupied in October 1886, while John built Ashley Bank House. By far the biggest cost incurred in building Erkinholme was the digging of the drive and approach road (Bar Brae) through the end of the Bar Wood. The gas to light these houses was produced at Waverley's own gas-works before being piped to each mansion. The original gas fittings are still in place at Erkinholme.

An entry for Ashley Bank House first appeared in the 1870-71 edition of *The Valuation Role for the County of Dumfries*, implying that the house was built shortly before this. However, the 1885-86 edition mentions that John Scott's house was being re-built, and this ties in with the construction of Ashley Bank Lodge, which was also built at this time. Clearly, a healthy rivalry existed between the two brothers as to who could build the finest mansion.

Alex and John Scott were generous patrons to many worthy causes in the town. Their benevolence helped to built the Mission Church (Mission Hall) and to install an organ in the Parish Church. Alex Scott also paid for the inscription on the wall of Langholm Library to mark its association with the great civil engineer Thomas Telford, and the strengthening of the ruins of the Auld Kirk up the brae when they seemed on the point of collapse. He was often seen to slip money into the hands of old deserving residents, and would supply coal and medicines to the needy. However, like most Borderers he had a strong dislike of all sham, was apt to be blunt and always spoke his mind. He took a particularly strong stance over the issue of betting at the Common Riding. He and his family were (and still are) extremely generous patrons of this great local festival, and when he died in May 1903, the Common Riding Committee felt it prudent, as a mark of respect and gratitude, to postpone the annual public meeting.

The Scott family were also generous employers and were held in high esteem by their workers. When young Tom Scott married in 1902, the family threw a massive party for all workers and friends in the fields behind Erkinholme. Shortly afterwards, to mark the Coronation of King Edward VII, they gave each worker the gift of 2/6d. In addition to this, and as an inducement to save, the apprentices were each given £1 and a bankbook, which had not to be touched until they reached the age of twenty-one.

In 1895, James Scott of Kilncleuch (known locally as "Jams"), the eldest son of John Scott and grandson of James Scott of the Claygate, built Kilncleuch Mill on the Holmfoot Park, slightly downstream from Waverley Mills and managed it for fourteen years. His brother Walter assisted him in this enterprise, and they traded under the name of 'James Scott' obviously hoping to exploit the high reputation of their neighbour, James Scott and Sons of Waverley Mills! This ploy caused great annoyance to their uncle, Alex who would no doubt make his feelings known to them! After passing through the hands of two other owners, 'the Bottom Mill', as it was known locally, was renamed Glenesk Mill when it was finally bought in 1919 by Robert G Neill from Earlston and his son, John. Soon afterwards, Andrew B Neill, Robert's other son joined the company, and John's son, R Kenneth Neill joined his father, grandfather and uncle in the business in 1930. After the war, the Company's trade was mainly in twist suitings of various weights, which were sold to merchants in the UK, Western Europe and Japan. In 1961, William (Bill) Neill Johnstone, John Neill's grandson, joined the company as a designer and became a director in 1964. The business was sold to the Illingworth Morris Group the following year for between £120,000 and £130,000. As a gifted designer in his own right, Bill Johnstone brought about a diversification in the business by moving from traditional men's suiting and jacket cloths into high-class ladies' wear, selling to companies like Jaeger and Aquascutum.

Sadly, after 103 years of producing high-class cloths, this famous old Langholm mill ceased production on 21st May 1998. The buildings were subsequently demolished and in their place Lothian, Borders & Angus Co-operative Society built a superstore which started trading in November 2000.

In 1985, Bill Johnstone left R G Neill's to set up his own designer-led textile company, Neill Johnstone, with partner Alex Graham, who had been a fellow director at Neill's Mill. Initially the business was housed in the top flat of Shaddon Mills in Carlisle but in 1988 it moved back to the town by leasing space from Reid & Taylor. Today, this prestigious company can claim amongst its customers such greats in the fashion world as Prada, Escada, Donna Karran, Daks, Valentino and Chanel. Tweed manufactured by the company featured in the Jean Muir spring/summer collection for 2003. The head designer of this world famous fashion house, Joyce Fenton-Douglas is another successful export of the Muckle Toon.

The Criterion Mill was situated on the south-east side of Waverley Mills, and was built in 1878 by Messrs Scott and Erskine. William Scott was yet another son of James Scott of Claygate and a brother to Alex and John. This mill was a much smaller establishment than the mighty Waverley, consisting of a small four roof-shed, 20hp engine, and a few power and handlooms. In 1888, the business was taken over by Arthur Bell, the son of John Bell who ran a woollen merchant's business from premises in the middle of the High Street. A fascinating relic of this old business still remains; for it is just possible to read the words "John Bell & Sons", which are painted on a door lintel at the rear of what were William Smith & Son's premises in the Pot Market (David Street).

In 1883, before buying the Criterion Mill, Arthur Bell started up on his own in a most unconventional way in premises in West Street. The only machinery he possessed were two handlooms for pattern making, all wool dyeing, spinning and weaving being done by commission. He was in effect "a spinner without spindles and a manufacturer without looms", but he was driven by the dream that he could make woollen cloth better, and more cheaply, than he could buy it. In 1888, he bought the empty Byers' Mill, off Buccleuch Square, but this venture proved to be short-lived as the Criterion Mill, complete with all its machinery, came on to the market that same year.

A year later, Byers' Mill was sold to R B Milligan who converted it into a theatre and dance hall, known locally as Milligan's or the Buccleuch Hall. The upper floor of this unique building was also the first meeting room for the local branch of The Salvation Army when that great religious body first came to the town between 110 and 120 years ago. Like so many buildings before it, it finally succumbed 'to the power of the flames' in a fierce and remarkably swift fire in January 1950, when Cairns of Langholm were using the building as a blanket factory.

Arthur Bell renamed his new premises Buccleuch Mill and greatly extended it. He ran the business as a small 'vertical company' rather than as a 'horizontal' one. Vertical companies performed all or most of the processing from raw wool to the finished fabric, whereas horizontal companies specialised in only one or two processes, passing the material on to other specialised companies, which handled those processes which they did not. To achieve this he built a carding and spinning unit at a cost of £6,000 in 1906, and added a dye house soon after this. The carding and spinning house was destroyed by fire in January 1914, but was rebuilt almost immediately.

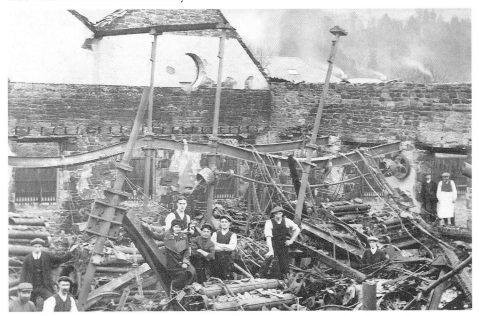

The aftermath of the 1914 fire which destroyed part of Arthur Bell's Mill

Arthur Bell died in February 1929, and was the last of the local 'tweed barons' to be buried in the serene grandeur of Wauchope Kirkyard. He was succeeded by his son, Major Edward J Bell, a Provost of the Burgh, who installed the electrical generating plant, making the mill self-sufficient in power from 1930 until the mid 1950s. By the end of the Second World War, the company was in a very weak position, caused in part by the severe taxation imposed during the war, and by a steep decline in the demand for hand tailoring. The production of military uniform cloths during the war had also caused heavy wear and tear on the ageing machinery, which was gradually replaced over the next couple of decades, and the modernisation brought vast improvements in both quantity and quality, despite a temporary setback when fire again destroyed the carding department in 1969.

The period from 1985 to 1989 was the most productive period in the mill's history when Arthur E I Bell, the founder's great grandson, ran the company with his son, Edward. The rationalisations they made involved closing the pattern shop and the buying of a Hergeth sample-warping machine, which allowed all ranges and samples to be woven in amongst normal piece production.

Passing out of family ownership, the Company was sold to a Yorkshire-based textile group, Yorklyde plc in the summer of 1988, exactly one hundred years after the founder had started his business on this same site. Despite large investments, the venture proved to be financially unviable for Yorklyde, and the company of Arthur Bell (Scotch Tweeds) closed its doors in July 2002, delivering another devastating blow to the local economy.

One ex-worker, Ian Ritchie summed up the sadness and frustration that many felt in a farewell to Bell's Mill.

> *'There's nae mair banter,*
> *And nae mair fun,*
> *Because for Bell's the race is run*
> *We were the best – it's no' oor blame,*
> *But that's no eneef – we've hed a' oor fame*
> *The hale thing is ower*
> *A hunder'-odd years*
> *It's a' geen to waste*
> *And ended in tears!'*

In its heyday, the mill's own dye works was large enough to handle all dyeing requirements in the town. However, in 1946 all dyeing ceased at the mill.

Andrew (Drew) Stevenson was the last foreman dyer at Arthur Bell's Mill. As a fourteen-year-old boy, he had served his apprenticeship with Turnbull the Dyers in Hawick, where his father was head dyer. On completing his indentures, he found himself in the enviable position of being offered three jobs, one in Selkirk, one in India and the third in Langholm. He chose the last and intended to stay for a couple of years before moving on again. Instead, he stayed for sixty-one years. He persuaded the owners of the local mills that there was now the need for a new, independent dyeing company in the town. So in 1947 he, along with Major E J Bell and G E Bell from Bell's Mill, Alex Scott and W Sutton Scott from James Scott & Sons and Percy Howard and Robbie R Scott-Hay from Reid and Taylor, built a joint dyeing company on a site at the riverside and called this new enterprise The Langholm Dyeing and Finishing Company. Drew Stevenson was appointed the Managing Director of this new company, which was supported by a start-up capital of £25,000 and had a total workforce of six people. In 1966 his son Neil, a dye chemist, entered the business and he succeeded his father as Managing Director in 1972. Mr Stevenson's eldest son, David joined the company in 1967 to handle the accountancy and selling side of the business. Initially the company dyed only raw wool and a small amount of fabric but Drew Stevenson became one of the pioneers of the technique of package dyeing, that is, the dyeing of yarn on cheeses or cones. The dyeing of loose wool was fraught with problems, as the chemical action of the dye tended to weaken the fibres, causing the wool to matt thereby making spinning difficult. An alternative method, dyeing yarn in hanks, also gave problems. Therefore, the Langholm Dyeing and Finishing Company experimented with the radically new technique of dyeing yarn on the cone, which made for better quality production and, significantly, better stock control as precise weights could be dyed. Despite years of scepticism in the industry elsewhere, local confidence in the new process could not be shaken, even though it would be thirty years before the technique was accepted nationally. The gamble paid off and the Langholm Dyeing and Finishing Company, the first commission package dyers in Great Britain, flourished.

In 1989, the business left local control when it was sold to the Leeds Group.

The modern dye works is a highly sophisticated operation involving totally enclosed microprocessor-controlled systems. As well as commission dyeing, where the customer supplies the raw yarn to be dyed, the company also produces a wide range of dyed yarns to sell to its clients. In December 2001, four directors were involved in a management buy-out of the company.

1973 saw the end of the Scott dynasty in Langholm when Alex Scott, the great-grandson of the founder, retired. The local firm of James Scott and Sons, which had been run by four successive generations of the same family for a record 108 years, ceased to be.

The Edinburgh Woollen Mill Ltd bought the empty Waverley Mills in 1975. David Stevenson had set this company up five years earlier with the sole purpose of running a shop in Randolph Place in Edinburgh. Soon afterwards, it merged with Langholm Woollen Crafts, which was born out of a one-day sale of 'factory seconds' skirt lengths at a shop on the dye works site. The Edinburgh Woollen Mill targeted those towns and cities in Scotland with year-round tourist trades such as Edinburgh, Ayr, Perth and Stirling. Its shops are geared towards the 'middle age plus' section of the day trip tourist market and sell a wide array of traditional Scottish products including woollens, skirts, tartans, rugs, sheepskin and leather products as well as the obligatory shortbread and fudge. The tartan and check materials they sell are woven at the company's own plant at Heather Mills in Selkirk. The tartan is then sent to The Jedburgh Kilt Maker's factory in Jedburgh to be made into kilts.

In 1993 the company acquired one of their biggest competitors, Grampian Woollen Mills (comprising Pitlochry Knitwear, Moffat Woollens and James Pringle Weavers), which gave it a valuable inroad into the lucrative Highlands market. In October 1996 the investment group, Grampian Holdings (which already owned a 25% stake in the company) bought the remaining 75% of the company's equity. In July 2001, the company was taken over by Rutland Fund Management Ltd which moved the entire distribution centre to a large site on the recently closed RAF 14 MU base at Kingstown in Carlisle. The administration, buying and design centres of the company have, however, remained in the town. The business changed hands again when management bought the business for £67.5 million in November 2002, and it is hoped that this will guarantee long-term employment to the 500 people currently employed in Langholm.

With over 285 outlets throughout the UK and Northern Ireland, employing a total workforce of 3,300, The Edinburgh Woollen Mill Group is undoubtedly one of the greatest success stories of the last twenty-five years in the Scottish retail trade.

In 1972, John Hammond from Winchester was touring in the Lake District and decided to 'put a toe into Scotland' by visiting the Scottish Border Country. On his way back south, the mists descended and he was forced to spend the night in bed and breakfast accommodation in Langholm. In the morning he was so struck by the beauty of the landscape and the warmth and friendliness of the people that he commented to his hosts that it would be "wonderful to live and work in this part of the world". Within three weeks he received a letter from them informing him that an ideal property had just come on the market – the eighteenth century farmhouse called Middleholms on the hillside just south of the town. Border Fine Arts started up the following year in the outbuildings behind this house with a total workforce of three.

The first figurines they produced were cast in silver or bronze, but John soon realised that what customers really wanted were hand-painted ceramic models. The company therefore began to experiment with a special cold casting process, an off shoot from the space industry, to produce detailed ceramic models, which could then be hand-painted by local artists. The workforce rocketed as the demand for these high quality figurines outstripped availability. The company moved to a new factory on the old railway station site in Langholm and, over the years, this was extended to take in the old gasworks site and the Band Hall on Drove Road, which is now St Francis Roman Catholic Church. The company also opened satellite factories in Carlisle, Northampton and Northern Ireland. In 1986 the company was honoured by winning the Scottish Business Achievement Award in recognition of its commitment to making quality products. The company has made several pieces for members of the Royal Family including an Aberdeen Angus Bull and Cruachan, a Silver Highland Pony, for the late Queen Mother, Colonel-in-Chief of the Argyll and Sutherland Highlanders. Pieces made for Her Majesty the Queen include a Cleveland Bay Stallion 'Forest Foreman', a Haflinger Horse and two 'balls' of Corgis and Dorgis (Corgi/Dachshund crosses) painted in the markings of Her Majesty's own dogs.

In 1994 the company was also commissioned to re-paint a Roe Buck and two Chamois, cast-iron sculptures from the grounds of Balmoral Castle. (The Roe Buck had fallen into disrepair after having been used for target practice!)

That same year, the company was sold to Enesco, the massive American giftware group which had ready access to well-established distribution channels throughout the world. Many Border Fine Arts figurines have become highly sought after collectors' pieces. Their loyal customers return to buy, time after time, knowing that the outstanding craftsmanship and attention to fine detail will never be compromised.

To mark the Jubilee of Her Majesty the Queen's Coronation in June 2003, the company released what must

The repainted Roe Buck from Balmoral Castle

be its most lavish limited edition figurine to date – the Gold State Coach. The figurine portrays the scene as The Queen and Prince Philip left Buckingham Palace for Westminster Abbey on the morning of her Coronation. The tableau depicts, in amazing detail, each of the eight horses, four postillions, eight walking grooms, six coachmen, four yeomen and one brakeman, which made up the royal procession, while the fabulously crafted State Coach is embellished with 24 carat gold plate.

9

Thomas Telford

Laughin' Tam Telford – 'The Colossus of Roads'

A dusty corner in Westminster Abbey is the resting place of Eskdale's most famous son – Thomas Telford, one of the greatest civil engineers this country has ever produced.

He was born the son of an 'unblameable shepherd' in a cottage up the Meggat Burn on the farm of Glendinning, Westerkirk in August 1757. Three months after his birth, his father died, leaving his widowed mother and her baby destitute. Thanks to the kindness of warm-hearted relatives, a room was found for them at a cottage at The Crooks, two and half miles down the valley, and it was here that his mother, Janet Telford spent the rest of her life.

'Laughin' Tam', as he was known because of his cheery and fun-loving nature, grew up as a herd on the neighbouring farms during the summer holidays from school, and was given his food, a pair of stockings and 5/- a year to buy clogs in return for his labours. Janet Telford was a proud and hard-working woman and, rather than be branded an 'alms-taker,' she paid her way in life by toiling beside her son on these farms, milking the ewes, making hay and shearing sheep.

It was his cousin, Thomas Jackson, the Factor at Westerhall Estate, who paid for the principal part of his education at Westerkirk Parish School. Although education was very basic, consisting of little more than reading, writing and figures, he learned the beginnings of a great deal. Telford shared this classroom with a number of other local boys who were to find fame out beyond the quiet Eskdale hills, including the two eldest sons of the Malcolm family, and Andrew Little who became a naval surgeon before settling down as a highly respected teacher in Langholm after he lost his eyesight at sea.

When Thomas reached the age of fifteen, it was felt that he should learn an honest trade and so was apprenticed to a mason in Lochmaben. However, this man was cruel to the boy and within a few months he was back home in Westerkirk. At this point his cousin, Thomas Jackson again came to his aid and arranged for the boy to complete his apprenticeship with Andrew Thompson, a mason in Langholm. He lived in Langholm while honouring his indentures and would often walk home to The Crooks on Saturday evenings to visit his mother and accompany her to the parish church of Westerkirk on Sundays. It was at this time that his horizons were widened considerably through a friendship he struck up with Miss

Elizabeth Pasley. This elderly Langholm lady, the aunt of Sir Charles Pasley, had the largest collection of books Tam had ever seen, and he was given free access to this remarkable store of literature. It was one book in particular, Milton's epic poem *Paradise Lost*, that triggered his great passion for poetry. He once remarked that "verse to me is what a fiddle is to others; I apply it to relieve my mind after being much fatigued with close attention to business". Telford became a noted rhymester in the homely style of Fergusson and Ramsay and, while still a young man, contributed verses to *Ruddiman's Weekly Magazine* under the pen name 'Eskdale Tam'. Being a good writer, he was often called upon by workmates and friends to write letters to distant members of their families, and in this way Telford learned all the tittle-tattle and social history of the town.

As a fully-fledged journeyman mason, earning only 18d a day, he worked on the new cottages of 'Good Duke Henry's' model village of New Langholm and with Robin Hotson on the construction of the Langholm Bridge, where he first learned the principles of bridge building. It is claimed that Telford left his mason's mark on a number of stones on the bridge. However, the mark found at the eastern end of the bridge, consisting of a triangle linked to a diamond by a short line, bisected by a cross, differs from the mark he used later in life.

The mark, which appears on later works, and on the memorial at Bentpath, is a double-headed arrow with a shaft bisected by a cross. It may be that the mark on the bridge is not his, or that he modified it slightly at a later point in his career.

In 1780 he left Eskdale and, with his belongings over his shoulder, made his way on foot up the Ewes road to Edinburgh. He stayed in Edinburgh for almost two years working as a mason on the fine Georgian buildings that were springing up on the north bank of the 'Nor' Loch, in Edinburgh's New Town. Every spare minute was put to good use studying architecture and the mysteries of plans and elevations. However, Telford had set his sights on bigger and better things. He longed to travel to London to study the architecture of its fine old buildings. Not being able to afford the coach fare, it happened that Sir James Johnstone, the Laird of Westerhall, needed a reliable person to deliver a horse to a member of his family in the Metropolis – so Tam volunteered immediately.

He returned briefly to Eskdale at the end of 1781, but only to say his farewells to family and friends. In January 1782, dressed in his cousin's buckskin breeches and bearing little more than a mallet, chisel, leather apron and a cheery disposition, he headed south for London … and world renown. Years later his cousin would tease Tam saying that he was very welcome to the loan of the horse, "but he micht hae sent him back the breeks!"

Telford masterminded some of the most ambitious and ingenious civil engineering projects this country has seen. The progress of the Industrial Revolution was being hampered by the abysmal state of the country's road and canal networks. No other engineer did more to improve the infrastructure of Britain than Telford. In the Highlands of Scotland alone, over a period of eighteen years, he built 920 miles of roads and 1,117 bridges. His good friend, the Poet Laureate, Robert Southey dubbed him 'The Colossus of Roads' because of these amazing feats of construction.

He built the Ellesmere Canal, which linked the Mersey, Severn and Dee, thus creating a waterway between Liverpool and Bristol, and the magnificent Saint Catherine's Dock in London, now a tourist attraction. Sir Walter Scott said that his aqueduct at Pont-Y-Cyssylte was "the greatest work of art he had ever seen". Telford also designed the highway between London and Holyhead, vastly improving communications with Ireland. This arterial road incorporated the huge, towering and beautiful suspension bridge over the Menai Straits, which links the island of Anglesey to the Welsh mainland. His fame spread to Europe; in Sweden he built the Gotha Canal and was rewarded with a Swedish knighthood. In Russia, he built the Warsaw frontier road for Tsar Alexander. Other examples of his work can be found in Austria, Poland and Germany.

The chair, books and bust of Thomas Telford in the Library of
The Institution of Civil Engineers, London

In his native Scotland, Telford is remembered for opening up the Highlands with his amazing network of roads and bridges, which still form the basis of the road system today. The existing roads had been allowed to fall into disrepair and were little more than rough cart tracks, many having been built as military roads by General Wade and his successors in the early part of the eighteenth century. In the south of Scotland, he built the highways from Carlisle to Glasgow and the Carter Bar road across the Cheviots to Edinburgh, by Soutra.

Telford also carried out a vast programme of harbour and dock construction on the northern and western coasts for the British Fishery Board. He oversaw the renovation or complete construction of harbours and docks at Wick, Peterhead, Fraserburgh, Banff, Nairn, Dingwall, Thurso, Fortrose and Kirkwall. By 1823 it was estimated that a sum in excess of £108,530 had been spent on these and other harbours. He also supervised the reconstruction of the harbours at Aberdeen, Dundee, Ardrossan and Glasgow.

In Edinburgh no bridge is more impressive than the one that he built across the Water of Leith, just downstream from the village of Dean. He also toyed with the idea of building a road bridge at Queensferry but, of course, it was to be another 133 years before this dream became a reality. However, his most impressive construction in Scotland was, without doubt, the Caledonian Canal – a masterpiece of the first industrial revolution. This canal, the largest in the world at the time, is 100ft wide and 20ft deep, and links Inverness with Fort William. Its construction effectively cut the Highlands in two, and offered ships a faster and more direct route from the North Sea to the Atlantic. Ironically, by the time it was partially completed in 1822 (at a cost of £1million) it had outlived its usefulness, as rail communication had all but rendered canal transport obsolete. However, it remains one of Telford's most enduring legacies.

In 1820, a group of young engineers met in a coffee shop in London to form a society, the aim of which was to promote engineering as a profession rather than as a trade operated by unskilled, illiterate workers. Telford was asked to be the first President of this Institution of Civil Engineers and he agreed with mock modesty to take the post "until a fitter person could be selected". He immediately made a gift of a collection of books, which was to form the basis of the Institution's extensive library. The patronage and financial support he gave this small, fledgling body was the major reason why it survived to become the great Institution that it is today.

The only remnant of Telford's own work remaining in Langholm is a stone archway in the old Library grounds, which was once the doorway to the King's Arms Inn. This old hostelry was situated where the Eskdale Hotel stands today. Only two other examples of his craftsmanship still exist in Eskdale. One is the simple headstone, which the dutiful son cut and placed over his father's grave in the old Churchyard at Westerkirk. On this stone is also inscribed the name of an older son, also called Thomas, who died in infancy. A few paces away is the other memorial by Telford, the grave of the Pasley family. The last to be buried there was Elizabeth Pasley, the Langholm lady who did so much to nurture young Tam's passion for literature.

In spite of all he achieved, Telford always remembered his humble beginnings as a simple stonemason in Langholm. During one of his visits home in 1795, he met an old friend and fellow stone mason called Frank Beattie. Beattie had abandoned the trade some years before and was now an Innkeeper (in fact it was he who built the Crown Hotel, and was later to become one of the 'Fathers of the Common Riding'). When Telford asked what had become of Beattie's mell and chisels, Beattie replied that they were "all dispersed – perhaps lost!" The great man then went on to say that all his tools were locked away along with his old working clothes in a room at Shrewsbury, just in case he ever needed them again.

In Westerkirk Churchyard stands this simple headstone, cut by
a dutiful son for his father

Nor did Telford ever forget the great kindness which was shown to him and his mother while he was a boy in Westerkirk. He would often take the time to enquire after families he knew, and each New Year would send between £30 and £50 to Miss Malcolm of Burnfoot, who would then distribute it among the needy of the valley.

All who knew Thomas Telford knew him as an immensely cheerful and generous host who valued the company of children as much as he did that of adults. On one occasion, a young boy was describing to Telford a friend who had achieved so many wonderful things. Telford listened politely, and then with a characteristic twinkle in his eye replied, "Pray, can your friend lay eggs?"

He placed little importance on personal wealth, and often refused to take payment for projects, which he felt benefited the country, particularly those in his native Scotland. He also had small regard for his own dignity, and to the end of his days retained the old working mason's practice of darning his own stockings.

Thomas Telford died at his home at 24 Abingdon Street, London, on the 2nd September 1834, after a violent attack of 'bilious derangement'. Despite severe pain, he had maintained his punishing schedule of work almost to the end. He never married, and had begun to spurn mixed company due to hearing problems. It was his wish that he should be buried, without ceremony, in the parish church of St Margaret in Westminster, but the Institution of Civil Engineers refused to honour this request. Westminster it was to be, but not a humble church – for this Eskdale lad was buried in the magnificent splendour of the Abbey itself, amid the greatest and best in the land.

His great legacy to this area was to leave £1,000 (which grew to the sum of £2,700 when the estate was finally settled) to each of Langholm and Westerkirk Libraries, to repay the kindness of those who had lent books to this humble shepherd's son.

Thomas Telford never forgot his beloved Eskdale, nor did Eskdale ever forget him. In August 1928, a handsome memorial was unveiled by the Duke of Buccleuch in the presence of the President and members of the Institution of Civil Engineers, along with Provost Cairns of Langholm and members of the Eskdale and Liddesdale Archaeological Society. This local society had been the driving force behind the project. The costs were met by donations, by far the largest amount coming from the Institution itself. The memorial, erected by Messrs Beattie and Co of Carlisle, was designed by Curtis Gray and was fashioned from grey granite from the quarries at Creetown. Originally it stood on the roadside a mile north of Bentpath, and overlooked the confluence of the Meggat Burn and the Esk. Today it stands in front of Westerkirk Library, which benefited so much from his generosity.

The most poignant tribute that can be paid is found in some lines that were penned by a man who never forgot the people and hills of his native Eskdale, despite all the fame and glory that the outside world had heaped upon him.

> 'Yet still one voice, while fond remembrance stays,
> One feeble voice, shall celebrate thy praise;
> Shall tell thy sons that, wheresoe'r they roam,
> The hermit peace hath built her cell at home;
> Tell them, Ambition's wreath, and Fortune's gain,
> But ill supply the pleasures of the plain;
> Teach their young hearts thy simple charms to prize,
> To love their native hills, and bless their native skies.'

Thomas Telford

Sir John Malcolm

'Big enough to walk alone'

Not far from Telford's memorial in Westminster Abbey is one to another distinguished son of Eskdale – Sir John Malcolm. But to Langholm folk the world o'er, this memorial pales into insignificance when compared with the one which crowns Whita Hill. For this stone obelisk, so beloved by Eskdale folk, is quite simply 'The Monument'. To them there is none better or grander on the face of this earth.

There are many, scattered throughout the world, who in a fleeting flight of fancy will gaze back in their mind's eye on that beloved spire and 'The Wee Bit Toon' that nestles beneath it, cradled in Whita's verdant bosom.

> *'Here my horizon is more vast –*
> *Beneath me in the valley lies the town,*
> *That in a native's eyes*
> *Possesses beauties unsurpassed'*
>
> Whita Hill Top – A Reverie
> by Matthew Welsh

The man who inspired it was the fourth of ten sons and seven daughters born to George and Margaret Malcolm of Burnfoot, Westerkirk. Of those ten boys, four were knighted for distinguished military service to their country and became known as 'The Four Knights of Eskdale'.

George was a boy when the Malcolm family first came to the area in 1717. The Earl of Dalkeith had offered his father, the Rev Robert Malcolm from Cupar in Fifeshire, the combined parishes of Nether and Over Ewes. To supplement his meagre stipend he was given the tenancy of a farm, Burnfoot (or Cannel Shiels as it was then called) in the neighbouring valley. George did not follow his father into the ministry, preferring to work the land instead. He married Margaret, the daughter of James and Magdalen Pasley who worked the neighbouring farms of Craig and Burn. Magdalen's great-grandfather on her mother's side was no less a person than Gilbert Elliot of Stobs (Gibbie o' the Gowden Garters) who rode with Buccleuch to rescue Kinmont Willie Armstrong.

John Malcolm was born on 2nd May 1769, a day after the Duke of Wellington's birth, and in the same year as the Duke's great adversary, Napoleon. His uncle, John Pasley, took this unruly, unremarkable boy when only twelve to London to be interviewed by the Directors of the East India Company. It was felt that a life abroad might cure the high-spirited Jock of his wild ways. When asked what he would do if he met the fierce Indian chief Hyder Ali, Sultan of Mysore he replied, "A wad oot wi' ma sword an' cut his heid aff". This blunt response so impressed the Directors that within the year he was aboard the "Busbridge" and heading for a new life in India. He became a cadet in the Indian Army at Madras, and received his first active service against Tipu Sultan, the dreaded "Tiger of Mysore". Malcolm's career began to blossom when his cool headedness and diligence during tense times were noticed by Lord Richard Wellesley, the Governor General of India, who later made him his private secretary.

John Malcolm is best remembered for the major part he played in the building of the Indian Empire both as a soldier and statesman, particularly

Sir John Malcolm
From a portrait in Langholm Town Hall

as an ambassador. In 1800, Lord Wellesley sent Malcolm as his envoy to Persia on an important diplomatic and trade mission. Due to his great success in this, he returned in 1808 and again in 1810, as Britain's first Ambassador to that country. Malcolm's last visit to Persia left such an impression on the Persian Prince that he presented him with a valuable sword and star, and made him a Khan and Sepahdar of his country.

General Malcolm received the honour of Knight Commander of the Bath in 1815 in recognition of the distinguished service he had given to his country. His brothers, James and Pulteney were also knighted

that year, while Charles received his title eight years later, in 1823. That four brothers were all knighted for distinguished military service to their country is a unique achievement, which has never been paralleled in the annals of British history.

In December 1817 Malcolm, as Commander of the third division of the army, played a prominent part in the celebrated battle of Mehidpur, when the army of Mulhar Rao Holkar was beaten and routed. Major-General Sir John Malcolm returned home to Britain in April 1822 and promptly received an annual allowance of £1,000 from the Directors of the East India Company in recognition of his outstanding services whilst in the Indian sub-continent. He fully intended to spend the rest of his life quietly in England but this was not to be, for in 1827 he was persuaded to accept the honourable position of Governor-General of

Bombay, a post he held for four years until 1831. John Malcolm left India heavily laden with all manner of distinctions and honours, from every class of society for the people of that country looked upon him not as a warrior and conqueror, but rather as a benefactor and valued friend. The European gentlemen of Bombay requested that he sit for a statue (later executed by Chantrey), which they erected in Bombay; the members of the Asiatic Society cast a bust of him to place in their library; while the native gentlemen of Bombay commissioned a portrait of him to hang in their public room. John Malcolm had certainly left his mark on the Indian Nation, for it was remarked in Parliament at the time that "he was a gallant officer, whose name would be remembered in India as long as the British flag is hoisted in that country".

As a scholar and writer he had a first-hand knowledge of the history and legends of both India and Persia, writing a number of noteworthy books including, *A Sketch of the Sikhs*, *A Life of Robert, Lord Clive*, and *A Memoir of Central India*. In 1829 he published a small volume of miscellaneous poems in which he described the grandeur of his native vale. It was Malcolm's translation of an old Persian legend, which inspired Matthew Arnold's epic Sohrab and Rustum, with its immortal lines:

> 'So, on the bloody sand, Sohrab lay dead,
> And the great Rustum drew his horseman's cloak
> Down o'er his face, and sate by his son.'

As David J Beattie recalls in *Lang Syne in Eskdale*, as a young boy at Westerkirk School, Jock, as he was known, was always getting into scrapes and trouble, and when any mischief was done the old schoolmaster would say, "I'll warrant Jock's at the bottom of it". Many years later when this mischievous boy had become a man of world renown, a parcel arrived at Westerkirk School containing two volumes of his *History of Persia*, and written across the flyleaf were the words "Jock's at the bottom of it".

On his return from India in 1831, he entered Parliament as the Member for Launceston. But this new career was comparatively short-lived for he died in Prince's Street, London in May 1833 after a long and glittering career and was laid to rest in St James's Church in Piccadilly. His last public engagement, in the Thatched House Tavern, had been to rally support to buy Abbotsford for the family of the late Sir Walter Scott, who ironically like Malcolm had died of paralysis. Soon afterwards it was decided that the sculptor Chantrey should be commissioned to create a fitting memorial to the man whom Wellington once described as being "big enough to walk alone" and that it should be placed in the sepulchral calm of Westminster Abbey. Over £2,300 were raised in donations from such famous names as the Pasha of Egypt and T Telford Esq.

The people of his native vale erected the Langholm Monument in his honour, the funds required to build it being raised by public subscription. Of the 188 people who subscribed, by far the largest single donation of £50 came from a gent who signed himself simply as "T.T." – this being the way in which Thomas Telford would sign letters he wrote home to friends in Eskdale.

Sir James Graham of Netherby, Provincial Grand Master of the Cumberland Lodges of Freemasons, laid the foundation stone amid scenes of great pomp on Wednesday 16th September 1835. Indeed the Masonic apron worn by him on that great day can still be seen in a glass case in Lodge Eskdale Kilwinning. By breakfast time the town was already abuzz with excitement, as all manner of folk descended on it from every airt: gentlemen in carriages, yeomen on horseback, visitors in gigs and carts and hundreds of humble, plaided country-folk on foot. A magnificent triumphal arch of evergreens bearing the honoured name 'Malcolm' spanned the road to the hill, while the principal inns were beautifully festooned with flowers and banners bearing the insignia of Freemasonry. Sir James Graham arrived in the town at eleven o'clock to be warmly received by the other Brethren outside the Town Hall. After this, they formed into ranks to begin the formal procession up the torturous face of Whita to the site of the ceremony. It was estimated that the total number taking part in this procession, including those who preceded and followed the Freemasons, was in excess of 3,000 souls, undoubtedly the greatest number of people ever seen on Whita at any one time! Once at the summit the company formed into a circle round the stone, while Sir James Graham placed an inscription into a cavity in the bottom stone which read,

> The first stone of an obelisk erected in honour of the late Major-General Sir John Malcolm GCB &c laid by Sir James Graham, Bart, on 16th September, 1835.

He also placed a number of 'indices' of that period into this cavity. The upper stone, which was suspended from a triangular rig, was then lowered into place with the usual Masonic honours and to the tune *God Save the King*. The Grand Master then declared the first stone to be "justly laid by square and level".

Sir James then delivered an eloquent address in which he spoke of the many services rendered by Sir John Malcolm to his King and Country, saying, "in short, he had with his sword written his name in imperishable characters in the annals of his country". A temporary platform had been erected above the foundation stone, and on it were such notable people as Sir Pulteney Malcolm, Sir James Malcolm and Colonel Charles Pasley, and their families. The procession, headed and followed by bands, descended from the hill by a less rugged route, which brought them back into the town from the north. Despite heavy rain, the Freemasons processed through all major streets before disbanding at the Town Hall just before three o'clock. Afterwards, a formal dinner took place in a spacious tent, which had been erected in the yard of the Salutation Inn. Three hundred people attended the event, which was presided over by Colonel Charles Pasley. A large number of eloquent toasts were proposed and duly honoured.

Within the space of a year Malcolm's monument was complete. Its chaste and beautiful appearance was said to mimic the obelisk that was erected to Nelson in Glasgow. One hundred feet high, it was designed by Robert Howe and fashioned from local stone. Mr Howe had been Clerk of Works at the Royal Engineers' School in Chatham. In 1825 he was made Professor of Practical Architecture there, under 'local boy' Lieutenant – Colonel Charles Pasley, who founded the school. The local builder, Thomas Slack, had developed such an ingenious way of lifting and moving the stone blocks that no external scaffolding was needed until they reached a height of 93ft above the ground. When the top stone was firmly in place, and the last man had been safely winched to the ground, the workmen pulled at the ropes attached to the pins that secured the scaffolding. Down it crashed – no one was hurt and not a mark was made on the Monument, and a great cheer rang out.

The grandmother of the local author David J Beattie was one of the children present on that great day. When the apex stone was still on the ground, before being winched into place, one girl slipped past the foreman mason and perched herself on top of it. She was soon chased off by the angry workman, but for the rest of her life she always boasted that she was the only woman in the world to have sat on top of Langholm Monument!

This monument to a great son of Eskdale was built entirely by local men so, in a way, it is as much a tribute to them as it is to the man it commemorates.

The Marble Man

Admiral Sir Pulteney Malcolm

For 162 years, a statue known locally as 'The Marble Man' has dominated Langholm High Street. It commemorates another of the Four Knights of Eskdale, Admiral Sir Pulteney Malcolm, a brother of Sir John Malcolm.

It was first erected in March 1842 in front of the Town Hall on the spot where the Mercat Cross had stood. Early on the morning of the unveiling, a band played through the streets to remind folk that a unique ceremony was to take place in the Market Place later that day. Despite the dirty state of the roads, caused by snow which had fallen during the night, a large crowd assembled in front of the Town Hall to watch the ceremony. At about one o'clock a procession headed by Sir James and Sir Charles Malcolm, and accompanied by a local band, arrived at the statue. The two Malcolm brothers accompanied by J Little Esq of Bombay, J Scott Esq of Barugh, J Connell Esq of Langholm and the Sculptor, David Dunbar then mounted the platform, which had been erected in front of the statue for the occasion. As the band struck up *Rule Britannia*, the cloth covering the statue was removed and the crowd gave three hearty cheers. Sir James briefly addressed the crowd and said that he need not express the gratification he felt at having witnessed two monuments erected to his two brothers, an honour which as far as he knew had never before been conferred by the people of England *[Britain?]* upon two brothers. He was sure that their children and children's children would remember with feelings of pride and gratitude the lasting honour which had been conferred upon their ancestors.

At three o'clock a formal dinner was held in the Crown Inn. Mr Harley Maxwell presided over the proceedings and toasts were given in succession to The Queen, Prince of Wales, Princess Royal and Queen Dowager, to the Army and Navy, to Miss Malcolm, to Colonel Pasley, to Admiral Sir Pulteney Malcolm, to Sir John Malcolm and to Thomas Telford. The last three toasts were drunk in silence.

A ball was held in the same room at eight o'clock that night, and it carried on to nearly four o' clock the next morning, as the men were so reluctant to leave the dance floor and company of the bonny lassies of Eskdale. At the same time, a second dinner was held in another room in the inn, and about forty men, who represented the principal tradesmen of the town, attended.

The statue, which is seven feet high, stands upon a pedestal of granite eleven feet high, and is made of the most durable Italian marble. The whole structure weighs in the region of ten tons. Mr Dunbar, the sculptor, had his workshop in George Street and spent two years there, working on the piece. This wooden shed later became 'The Wud Kirk', the first Free Church in Langholm. Mr Dunbar was keen to let people examine the piece as he worked. He placed an advert in *The Dumfries Times* of August 1841, stating that locals would be admitted to his workshop in George Street each Wednesday from ten o' clock until dusk, while strangers would be admitted every "lawful day", on request.

The statue shows Sir Pulteney in the costume of a British Admiral; his left hand rests upon the hilt of his sword while his right hand rests on the Orders of Saint Michael and Saint John, which appear on his breast. All who knew Sir Pulteney said that the likeness was admirable!

The Marble Man in the Library Gardens during his re-siting

However, the scenes of jubilation which accompanied the unveiling of the statue were completely overshadowed by the acrimonious incidents surrounding the Admiral's removal to the Library Gardens forty-four years later. By the late summer of 1886 rumours were rife in the town that the Road Trustees were planning to evict the Admiral to make more room for stalls on market days. This met with a torrent of local opposition. A public meeting was held in the Temperance Hall where a formal protest was read out. Strong words of condemnation appeared in the local paper and an interdict was presented to the Court of Session in Edinburgh to block the removal ... but all to no avail. One local worthy, who wrote under the pen name Willie Wud, published a poem in the local paper in June 1886 called *The Admiral's Appeal* telling of the fateful night when 'The Marble Man' spoke out and begged to be left where he was!

'O Eskdale Lads, where'er ye be,
At hame or far beyond the sea,
At my request can ye do less,
Than help an auld frien' in distress;
For there's a rumour got abroad
That a just stan' here in the road,
And wants me moved frae this place here,
Where I've stood nearly fifty year.
Some wants me hid as dark as night,
In yon stray corner oot o' sight.

If they should shift me frae the cross,
How many a lively scene I'll loss.
Full forty times, and twa-three mair,
I've heard them cry the Langholm Fair.
As many times, close by my side,
I've seen the Cornet in his pride,
Waving his banner, proud man he,
Followed by prancing steeds that neigh,
To martial air, old yet unworn
That led the Scots at Bannockburn.'

The preparations to move the Admiral to "yon stray corner oot o' sight" carried on unabated. There was, however, an incident that would have brought a smile to the faces of the protestors. One day in early September, as the new pedestal was being built, one of the guy ropes that held the crane in place, suddenly snapped causing the equipment to topple. The massive stone it was carrying hit the ground with a resounding thud and broke in two. However, this proved to be only a temporary setback.

The Marble Man has stood in the Library Gardens for the last 118 years, and during that time has taken everything that the elements and the young folk of the town can throw at him! Over the years he has been forced to wear hats and dresses and has had rude things drawn onto his anatomy. In recent years he has been given a complete overhaul and has been turned round so that, were it not for the Town Hall, he would be gazing upon the scene he originally saw ... Langholm High Street stretching out towards the hills of his beloved Eskdale.

The first re-siting of The Marble Man

Pulteney Malcolm was born on the 21st February 1768, the third son of George and Margaret Malcolm of Burnfoot, Westerkirk. He joined the Navy at the tender age of ten to serve as a midshipman aboard the "Sybille" frigate, which was commanded by his uncle, Captain Pasley, later to become Admiral Sir Thomas Pasley, Bart. He accompanied him to the Cape of Good Hope and on returning followed his uncle onto the "Jupiter", which formed part of the squadron under

Commodore Johnstone, which was involved in the affair of Porto Praya and in the capture of a fleet of Dutch Indiamen in Saldanha Bay. Moving steadily up through the ranks he served under Lord Nelson during the Battle of Cadiz, but much to his dismay missed the Battle of Trafalgar as his ship was forced to have an emergency re-fit in Gibraltar at the time. With Herculean effort the "Donegal" was hastily made seaworthy again and, still dragging her foreyard alongside, she successfully navigated the Straits of Gibraltar in a heavy westwardly gale and arrived in time to capture the 120-gun Spanish ship "El Rayo" in the aftermath of the battle.

In 1806, he commanded the "Donegal" at the Battle of San Domingo in the West Indies when the French fleet was defeated by Sir John Duckworth, and it is worth noting that the corner posts of the rail around the memorial are replicas of the cannons on that ship. As thanks for the heroic part he had played in this battle, he was presented with a gold medal and the grateful thanks of both Houses of Parliament. He also received a handsome vase in recognition of the part he played in rescuing the crew of the foundering "Brave" on the homeward voyage.

Sir Pulteney is best remembered for the fact that in the spring of 1816 he became Commander-in-Chief of the Cape Station, which included the remote Island of St Helena, and as such guarded Napoleon after his defeat at Waterloo.

Napoleon was no model prisoner; he took a dislike to Sir Hudson Lowe Governor of the Island, who, he thought, did not treat him properly. However, a warm friendship sprang up between him and the Admiral and they had many interesting conversations. Many of these are recorded in a book entitled *A Diary of St Helena*, supposedly written by Lady Malcolm, but in all probability she only wrote down what the Admiral dictated to her. The Admiral was held in such high esteem by Napoleon that the latter is reputed to have said, "There is a man with countenance really pleasing, open, frank and sincere ... his countenance bespeaks his heart, I am sure he is a good man. He carries his head erect and speaks out openly and boldly what he thinks, without being afraid to look you in the face at the same time". On one occasion, while in a particularly black mood, Napoleon snapped at the Admiral, "Does your Government mean to detain me upon this rock until my death's-day?" The Admiral replied, "Such, I apprehend, is their purpose". "Then," said the ex-Emperor, "the term of my life will soon arrive". "I hope not," said Malcolm, "I hope you will survive to record your great actions, which are so numerous, and the task will insure you a term of long life". Napoleon's mood warmed to this compliment, he bowed graciously to the Admiral and said no more.

In 1821 Malcolm was advanced to the rank of Vice-Admiral, and seven years later was appointed as Commander-in-Chief of the Mediterranean. In 1837 after a long and illustrious career, Sir Pulteney was finally raised to the distinguished rank of Admiral.

Pulteney Malcolm's home in Eskdale was at Irvine House (formally known as Peel Holm), just a few miles south of Langholm. However, he died at East Lodge, Enfield, on the 20th July 1838, leaving one son, the much revered William Elphinstone Malcolm of Burnfoot. The Admiral was laid to rest in the Church of St Mary-le-Bone in London. Four years later a statue by the sculptor Bailey was erected to his memory in St Paul's Cathedral, adjacent to the monument to Earl St Vincent. The cost of £1,000 was met by subscriptions from the Admiral's many friends and admirers.

It has been said that a prophet has no honour in his own country, but in the case of the Malcolm brothers we may safely reverse this maxim for they were as much revered at home as they were honoured and distinguished abroad. An incident occurred in July 1822, which illustrated the level of esteem in which they were held in Langholm. The three brother Knights, Sir James, Sir John and Sir Pulteney were guests of honour at a lavish banquet held in the Crown Inn. When they came to leave, some members of the crowd, which had gathered in the street outside, unhitched the horses from their carriage and pulled it and its passengers through the streets and out of the town.

The Poets of Eskdale

Just as Eskdale has produced more than its fair share of military figures, it has also produced more than its fair share of eminent writers and poets who have found fame beyond the circle of its quiet hills.

Henry Scott Riddell

The author of that epic ballad *Scotland Yet* Henry Scott Riddell, was born three miles north of Langholm in a shieling on the farm of Sorbie on 23rd September 1798 and was christened in the old Kirk of Nether-Ewes. Two years later his father, Robert Riddell, was moved by his employer to an 'out-bye herding' in the wilds of Eskdalemuir

at Langshawburn. In his autobiography Riddell recalls that when he was "able to traverse both burn and brae, hill and glen," he frequently returned on foot to the "vale of his nativity" for many weeks at a time. While at Langshawburn, the family had many famous visitors including Sir Pulteney Malcolm and James Hogg, the Ettrick Shepherd. It was during these occasions when "the sons of farmers, and even of lairds mingled delightedly with the lads that wore the crook and plaid", that he started to store up large numbers of old Border ballads and songs. Hogg's mother, Meg Laidlaw of Ettrickhall Farm, was what modern scholars call a 'Tradition-bearer'; she could recite or sing vast numbers of Border stories and ballads. Much of the material, which appeared in Scott's *The Minstrelsy of the Scottish Border,* came from her or women like her, although she was critical of the work saying, "The sangs were made for singing, no' for prenting … they're no' setten doun richt nor prentit richt". Hogg inherited this great treasury of Border folklore from his mother, and would have entranced his audience with these tales as they sat round the cosy ingle neuk at Langshawburn. Riddell possessed a remarkable memory for songs. He said, "I could, on hearing a song, or even a ballad, sung twice, have fixed it on my mind word for word". In manhood the two became great friends (despite an age difference of twent-six years) and Hogg called Riddell "his assistant and successor".

While at Langshawburn, Robert Riddell employed a person to teach his children and those of a neighbouring shepherd, for several winters. However, Henry's education was spasmodic to say the least; the family was either too far from the nearest school to make the journey possible in bad weather, or it was that their tasks around the farm had to take precedence over learning. Like most boys, Henry was more interested in football, fishing and guddling than books and schoolwork. He was strong, agile, and always ready for mischievous fun, and at shows, fairs, and clippings, his athletic powers were always to the fore.

At the age of twelve he became a shepherd on the farm of Deloraine in Ettrick and then at Glencotha, in Holmswater, and finally at West Buccleuch where he was a lamb herd. He had a great deal of free time on his hands as he tended his flock on the lonely hillsides, and it was then that he started to apply himself to the task of self-improvement. He developed a voracious appetite for books, reading widely in all subjects and never went to the hill without tucking a book of some kind under the folds of his plaid. He became interested in archaeology, making excavations in the lonely churchyard at Rankleburn, and kept wild birds such as hawks, owls and ravens.

It was at this time that he made his first attempts at rhyme. He would sit on the lonely hillsides and, using his knee as a desk, would capture his thoughts and feelings on scraps of paper, which he would store under his hat. On more than one occasion, the wind blew his hat off, and these treasured scraps were scattered to the four winds.

It was while he was a shepherd at Todrigg on Alewater that he fell in with the farmer's son, Willie Knox. He shared Henry's passion for the muses and, in later life, became a renowned poet in his own right, having strong ties with the Ewes valley. However, Willie also had a passion for strong drink, and Riddell would often have to carry him home after wild drinking binges in the taverns of Hawick.

The idyllic life as a shepherd and bard among the quiet, green border hills suddenly changed when his father died unexpectedly. In his will he left Henry a small sum of money which he decided to put to good use by improving his education, enrolling at the Parish School in Biggar where he received an excellent grounding in classical subjects. After this, he entered Edinburgh and St Andrews Universities where he studied Philosophy. On completing university, he decided his future life lay in the ministry. Shortly after becoming a probationer, he was appointed to the new parish of Teviothead, south of Hawick. When the regular preacher died, the Duke of Buccleuch appointed Henry as his successor. It was at Teviothead that Riddell was to spend the rest of his life. With a meagre stipend of only £52 per annum and no manse available to him, he was forced to rent the farmhouse of The Flex, which lay nine miles from the church. He could not afford to keep a horse, and so had to walk the eighteen miles to church and back every Sunday – often cold and wet to the skin. However, in time the Duke did relent and built Teviothead Cottage as his manse in the parish.

It was while at The Flex that his wife gave birth to their second son, William, in December 1835. He, like his father, showed great promise as a poet and by the age of fourteen had written *The Lament of Wallace* which found its way into several collections of Scottish Minstrelsy. It was said that his rendering of his father's *Homily* in Cross Wynd Church, Hawick was one of the most sublime treats ever enjoyed in the town. Tragically he died at the age of twenty before his potential as a great poet could be fully realised.

In 1841 Henry Riddell was struck down with "that most dreadful of all maladies – insanity", after a cruel and groundless report caused him great distress and unhinged his mind. He spent a period in the Crichton Royal Asylum in Dumfries where he was a patient of the eminent Dr W Browne. After three years of treatment he made a complete and permanent recovery, although he never returned to the pulpit. Instead, he retired on a pension granted by the Duke, who also allowed him to retain the cottage at Teviothead and a small parcel of land around it. He spent the rest of his days as a recluse, only rarely appearing in the 'poets' corner' of some local newspaper or as a lecturer in some neighbouring town. He was finally at ease with the world and completely content with his lot. He continued to produce great works, in both prose and poetry, and always vowed that he could compose best when he had a hoe, spade or rake in his hand.

During a visit to Dumfries he was introduced by a mutual friend to Jean Armour, the widow of Robert Burns. At first Mrs Burns was uncommunicative and reserved. After her husband's death she was plagued with hordes of 'sightseers' and this may have explained her initial indifference towards the poet. However, in time she warmed to her visitor and began to tell him much about her husband, showing him many relics that she had retained. When he came to leave, she grasped his hand warmly and said that of all the men she had met, he bore the strongest resemblance to her husband.

Henry Scott Riddell died in his cottage at Teviothead on 30th July 1870. Three days later, surrounded by a great concourse of friends and admirers from far and near, he was laid to rest in the Kirkyard at Teviothead. Riddell's memorial stands next to that of Johnnie Armstrong; how appropriate that two men who have fired the imagination of many should lie close to each other in this small kirkyard.

Henry Scott Riddell wrote over two hundred poems and songs, including *The Wild Glens sae Green, Song of the Ark* and *The Crook and the Plaid*. He also translated the *Gospel of St Matthew* and *The Psalms* into Lowland Scots for Prince Louis Lucien Bonaparte, and wrote articles for the farming press and Hawick Archaeological Society. However, to this generation he is remembered solely as the author of that great patriotic ballad *Scotland Yet*, which still stirs the passion in countless breasts! It is said that he found the inspiration to write it while staying at Ramsaycleuchburn, at Teviothead, with his mother and brother. On waking one morning, after a particularly stormy night, he found that every facet of nature was fresh and clean, and the Ewesen Burn (which at this point falls through a rocky gorge and tiny series of waterfalls) was tumbling wildly and recklessly down the hillside. Inspired by what he saw, he returned to the cottage and wrote, without effort, the first draft of *Scotland Yet*. He read it aloud to his mother, who praised it greatly – the sweetest praise he had ever heard!

> 'Gae bring my guid auld harp ance mair,
> Gae bring it free and fast,
> For I maun sing anither sang
> Ere a' my glee be past.
> And trow ye as I sing, my lads,

The burden o't shall be—
Auld Scotland's howes, and Scotland's knowes,
And Scotland's hills for me;
We'll drink a cup tae Scotland yet,
Wi' a' the honours three.

The heath waves wild upon her hills,
And, foaming frae the fells,
Her fountains sing o' freedom still,
As they dance down the dells;
And weel I lo'e the land, my lads,
That's girded by the sea;
Then Scotland's vales, and Scotland's dales,
And Scotland's hills for me;
We'll drink a cup tae Scotland yet,
Wi' a' the honours three.'

That day he set out over the hills to visit his friend, James Hogg. At Hogg's house, he was introduced to a literary gent from London who had come to ask Hogg for a letter of introduction to Peter McLeod, the composer in Edinburgh. Hogg persuaded Riddell to write this letter instead, and with it he sent a copy of *Scotland Yet*. Mr McLeod was so taken with the poem that he immediately set it to music. The song became an instant hit in Edinburgh, and the profits from selling the music were given toward the cost of erecting iron railings around Burns' Monument on Calton Hill.

Henry Scott Riddell's Memorial stone on the A7 at Sorbie Hass road-end

In connection with the song, the question has often been asked, "What are the honours three?" The commonly held view is that they are the Scottish Regalia or Crown Jewels – the crown, sceptre and sword of Scotland, which Sir Walter Scott helped to recover from Edinburgh Castle in February 1818. Their re-discovery caused widespread rejoicing throughout the kingdom, and this would have fired young Riddell's fertile imagination.

In 1874, Hawick Archaeological Society and Masonic Lodge No 111 raised a fifty foot high stone cairn to his memory on Dryden Hill. Twenty-four years later, this same Masonic Lodge placed a memorial tablet above the door of his cottage at Teviothead. It bears the inscription "Here lived and died Henry Scott Riddell, author of Scotland Yet".

Although Riddell was known as 'The Bard of Teviotdale', the folk of Eskdale look upon 'their own' with special pride. In 1928, Sir George Douglas, the well-known authority on Border literature and poetry, unveiled a plaque on the wall of the bridge at Sorbie Hass road-end (under the auspices of The Eskdale and Liddledale Archaeological Society) in memory of the great man.

Each year, as the last Friday in July draws nigh, Eskdale folk sing with pride that great patriotic air and in doing so 'drink a cup' to the memory of our very own 'border minstrel' – Henry Scott Riddell.

Matthew Welsh

The Ewes valley has been the spawning ground for more than one poet of repute. Matthew Welsh was also born "where the Ewes gurgles doon" and like Riddell spent his boyhood days as a herd. He was born in September 1831 at Sandyhaugh on the Arkleton Estate. The cottage has been rebuilt, but at the time of his birth it was little more than a hovel as he describes in one of his poems: –

> 'Its timbers are rotten and frail,
> And bulging and bent is its wall,
> A terror in every gale, yet I tell no disastrous tale,
> It's weathered them all!'

Like Riddell, Welsh attended the parish school when he could, but by the age of eight was already herding cattle to subsidise his father's meagre wage. He reached a painful crossroads in his life in January 1849 when his father, Matthew, died. He had to decide either to develop the talents he had for literature and science by furthering his education elsewhere, or to stay at home and support his widowed mother. He chose the latter, and stayed in the employment of Mr Scott–Elliot for the whole of his working life. Again like Riddell, Welsh spent every spare moment with his head buried in some book or other. He particularly loved poetry, and his chief joy was original composition. He published a volume of his own work entitled *Maggie Elliot, A Romance of the Ewes and other Poems*, which received good reviews and sold well. The main poem *Maggie Elliot* is based on the legend of a love tragedy that happened in the Ewes valley five centuries ago. The piece tells how an Elliot Chief, Walter of Arkleton, captured the son of his mortal enemy, Foster of Cumberland, and intended to hold the boy for ransom. On returning to his keep, he handed the prisoner over to his daughter, Maggie who was to be his custodian. However, the unthinkable happened and the two fell desperately in love. Elliot had hoped that his daughter would marry the son of Scott of Harden (an ancestor of the Buccleuch family) and when he discovered the romance, he set out in a blind rage to halt this treachery. The two lovers fled to a spot near a deep pool in the Ewes nearby. It was mid winter and ice covered the surface of the water. In desperation they tried to cross but, alas, the ice was too thin to bear their weight and they both drowned in the freezing waters below.

> 'They reached the Ewes, just where its swollen tide,
> Chafing against the bank's steep, rocky side,
> Had scooped a dark, deep pool, this night the frost
> Had bridged it o'er, no moment to be lost.
> They tried to cross it o'er; but when midway –
> O cruel fate! – the fragile bridge gave way –
> A crash, an icy plunge, an iron grasp,
> A struggle, and a deep convulsive gasp,
> That lasted but a few short moments, then
> The lovers were beyond the reach of pain.'

Their bodies were discovered by Lady Boodle, an old wandering woman who lived in a cave nearby; she had been a mentor and friend to the young girl and had taught her the Gospel, pointing out how it rebuked the futile and barbarous warfare of clan with clan. Next morning Elliot came across the tragic, entwined lovers lying in Lady Boodle's arms. She accused him of making this "Peerless jewel" (his daughter) into a "stepping stone to thy ambition". He retorted that she had killed the young lovers and brandishing his sword, he smote her down with a mighty blow. However, retribution was close at hand, for Foster and his men had arrived at Arkleton to rescue his son. Elliot and his men fought valiantly against overwhelming odds, but in the end he died as he had lived – by the sword. When Foster discovered the bodies of the lovers, he ordered that they should remain together in death. A grave was dug and the lovers and their old friend were laid to rest by the banks of the Ewes.

> 'There by the crystal Ewes the trio sleep,
> While o'er their nameless grave the willows weep,
> And Ewes in mournful numbers, soft and low,
> Their requiem sings as past its waters flow.'

Welsh was a staunch member of the North United Free Church in Langholm, later known as the 'Toon Heid' or Erskine Kirk, and for twelve years had held Bible classes for young women in the congregation, walking the six miles from his house to the church and back every Sunday.

Matthew Welsh finally left Arkleton in his seventieth year. He retired to Langholm where he spent his days writing and studying the archaeology and folklore of the area, of which he was a great authority. By the time he died at Park House, Broxburn in February 1926, he had served as an elder of that church for over fifty years.

William Knox

William Knox was another poet who had a tangible connection with the Ewes valley. He was born on the farm of Firth, near Lilliesleaf in the neighbouring shire of Roxburgh and was educated at Lilliesleaf Parish School and then at the Grammar School in Musselburgh. In 1812 Knox, then twenty-three years old, came as a tenant to the small farmstead of Wrae two miles north of Langholm. The five years he spent there were not by all accounts particularly successful ones. He did, however, write *The Lonely Hearth* while at the Wrae and this poem brought him friendships with Sir Walter Scott and Henry Scott Riddell. He finally settled in Edinburgh two years later. Like Scotia's Bard, Robert Burns, he had a comparatively short life, dying in the Scottish capital at the age of thirty-six.

Knox, like Riddell, is solely remembered for a single classic work – *Mortality* which became a great favourite of President Abraham Lincoln of America who would recite it in public whenever the opportunity arose. In fact, it was so closely associated with Lincoln that many Americans thought that he had written the poem himself. It was also a great favourite of the Emperor of Russia, Tsar Alexander II, who had it printed in gold letters onto a cloth, which hung in one of the state rooms of his palace. The poem opens with its famous verse: -

> '*Oh! Why should the spirit of mortal be proud?*
> *Like a swift, fleeting meteor, a fast flying cloud,*
> *A flash of the lightning, a break of the wave,*
> *He passes from life to his rest in the grave.*

and continues ...

> '*The hand of the king that the sceptre hath borne,*
> *The brow of the priest that the mitre hath worn,*
> *The eye of the sage and the heart of the brave,*
> *Are hidden and lost in the depths of the grave.*
>
> *The peasant, whose lot was to sow and to reap,*
> *The herdsman, who climbed with his goats up the steep,*
> *The beggar, who wandered in search of his bread,*
> *Have faded away like the grass that we tread.*
>
> '*Tis the wink of an eye, 'tis the draught of a breath,*
> *From the blossom of health to the paleness of death,*
> *From the gilded saloon to the bier and the shroud,*
> *Oh! Why should the spirit of mortal be proud?*'

William Julius Meikle

William Julius Meikle (Mickle) was another local poet who found fame out beyond the quiet hills of Eskdale. He was the third son of the Rev Alexander Meikle who came to the parish as Minister in 1717. His church, the first to be built in Langholm, was sited on steep pastureland behind Drove Road, and overlooked the town. Today, all that remains of Langholm Auld Kirk (which was built in 1703 and rebuilt in 1747 and again in 1779) is a portion of the gable and belfry, which survived the terrible storm of February 1948.

William Julius Meikle was born at Langholm in September 1734. He and his three brothers and three sisters spent their childhoods at their home, the Parish Manse of Langholm. This house, known as 'The Waas' (Walls), was built on the site of, and with stone from, Wauchope Castle, which at one time had belonged to the Dean of the Knights Templar. This Manse was situated to the south west of the existing manse (now called Springhill), which was erected in 1793. However, it has also been claimed that the Manse in which he was born was situated in the middle of Langholm, where The Royal Bank of Scotland now stands, although Hyslop in *Langholm As It Was* favours the site in Wauchope.

He attended Langholm Parish School, where he displayed a great taste for literature and poetry. It was probably at this time that he dropped the 'e' from his surname to conform with the local pronunciation. In the eighteenth century, spelling was very variable. For example, the Burnes family from the Mearns in Kincardineshire dropped the 'e' from their name to become Burns, when they moved to Ayrshire.

When he was fifteen the family moved to Edinburgh, where he attended the High School for two years. Incredible as it may seem, his first job when only sixteen, was as a clerk in a Brewery in the city. It transpires that his father had fallen heir to this Brewery and in time he passed the business on to his son. Unfortunately, William's heart was not in the job. His mind ran more on Homer or Virgil than on commerce, and he soon found himself bogged down in a financial morass. He was forced to borrow money from a friend to pay off his mounting debts, but it was not long before his creditors were back banging on his door. To avoid imprisonment for debt there was only one avenue left open to him – and that was to flee Edinburgh. Therefore, in 1763, he walked to Newcastle and then sailed down to London on a collier, arriving friendless and penniless. Later Mickle moved to that great city of learning – Oxford, not as a lecturer in one of its great 'temples of learning', but rather as a humble corrector of manuscripts for the Clarendon Press. It was in Oxford that he spent the rest of his life and produced his greatest works.

Mickle's translation of that epic poem *Os Lusiados* or *The Lusiad* won praise from the literati of the day. This massive work was written in the sixteenth century by Luiz Vaz de Camoens, the 'Homer of Portugal', and describes the commercial expansion of the Lusitanians (or Portuguese) from the time of Vasco Da Gama. What Pope did for Homer, Mickle did for Camoens with a zest and fire, which can be judged from the lines which form the beginning of the real narrative: –

> 'Now far from land, o'er Neptune's dread abode
> *The Lusitanian fleet triumphant rode:*

Onwards they traced the wide and lonesome main,
Where changeful Proteus leads his scaly train
The dancing vanes before the Zephyrs flowed,
And their bold keels the trackless ocean plowed;
And plowed before, the green-tinged billows rose
And curled and whitened round the nodding prows.'

The cost of printing the book was met by public subscription. The list of over five hundred subscribers included many eminent professors from Europe's great seats of learning. Also listed were a number of familiar names from nearer home including Captain Sir Thomas Pasley, John Maxwell Esq of Broomholm, The Duke of Buccleuch and James Johnstone Bart of Westerhall.

The unveiling of the memorial plaque on Langholm Town Hall
to W J Mickle by Sir George Douglas in 1925

The translation was an immediate success and earned Mickle £1,000. It also gave him a definite standing as one of the leading literary men of his age. It was at this time that he began a twelve-year friendship with the great lexicographer and critic, Dr Samuel Johnson and his biographer, Boswell.

In 1779 his relative George Johnstone, a former Governor of South Carolina, was given the command of "HMS Romney" and made Commodore of his squadron. Mickle sailed with him as his secretary. When the squadron docked at Lisbon he was received with great honours by Prince Don John of Braganza, the uncle of the Queen of Portugal, who had him elected as a member of the Portuguese Royal Academy.

The crew of any British ship which captured an enemy vessel was entitled to a share in the value of the ship (when condemned and sold), any cargo it carried and the bounty on enemy seamen taken as prisoners. This was known as 'prize money'. On returning home, Mickle found that his share of the prize money allotted to the squadron was enough to settle all his debts and make him secure for life. Despite all the honours heaped upon him, Mickle remained modest and unassuming. It was said that if he were asked if he was any relation of the celebrated translator of Camoens he would reply truthfully, "They were of the same family".

After relinquishing his post at the Clarendon Press to become a book reviewer, he settled down at Wheatley in Oxfordshire, where he wrote *Cumnor Hall*, his most popular work. This book inspired Sir Walter Scott to write his great romantic piece *Kenilworth*. In fact it was Scott's intention to call the book *Cumnor Hall*, but at his publisher's insistence it was changed.

If William Julius Mickle had written nothing else, he would still have found immortality as the author of that spirited, homely lyric *There's nae luck aboot the hoose*, also known as *The Mariner's Wife*, which Robert Burns described as being "worthy of the first poet".

For a long time a question mark hung over the authorship of this great Scots song. Some claimed the real author was the Greenock schoolmistress, Jean Adams. However, the overwhelming weight of evidence rests with Mickle, for the song was printed in an early edition of his works, and the editor had no doubt as to its authenticity. The controversy probably arose because it seems out of keeping with the rest of Mickle's more scholarly works, with its happy, rollicking chorus: -

> 'For there's nae luck aboot the hoose,
> There's nae luck at a';
> There's little pleasure in the hoose,
> When our gudeman's awa.'

It is ironic that his last poem, *Eskdale Braes*, written only a few weeks before his death, should hark back to the start of his life when, as a young boy, he delighted in wandering over the hills of his native Eskdale.

> 'By the banks of the crystal stream'd Esk,
> Where the Wauchope her yellow wave joins,
> Where the lambkins on sunny braes bask,
> And wild woodbine the Shepherd's bower twines.
>
> Maria, disconsolate maid,
> Oft sigh'd the still noon-tide away,
> Or by moonlight all desolate stray'd
> While woeful she tun'd her love-lay;
>
> Ah, no more from the banks of the Ewes,
> My shepherd comes cheerily along,
> Broomholm and the Deanbanks refuse,
> To echo the plaints of his song.'

The poet died at his home at Wheatley in October 1788, leaving a widow and one son. His body was laid to rest in the picturesque graveyard at Forrest Hill, where the inscription on his grave reads: -

> 'Mickle – who made the strong poetic tide
> Rule o'er Britannia's shores in Lusitanian pride.'

On 27th June 1925, at the instigation of the Townhead Literary Society, the late Sir George Douglas unveiled a granite tablet to his memory on the façade of Langholm Town Hall.

13

Hugh MacDiarmid

MacDiarmid – 'The New Makar of Scotland'

One local poet has attracted more attention and generated more controversy than any other, Christopher Murray Grieve or Hugh MacDiarmid, considered by many to be the greatest Scots lyric poet of the twentieth century.

The rift that developed between him and his contemporaries in the town was probably due to his extreme political views and outspokenness. He is surely the only person to have been expelled from the Communist Party for being a Nationalist, and from the Scottish National Party for being a Communist!

His childhood, like that of most other boys, was spent dookin' and guddlin', making islands in the Esk, gathering hines (wild raspberries) in the Langfauld, sledging on the Lamb Hill, or gathering nuts and crab-apples in the Scrog Nut Wud. He was born at 9.30 am on 11th August 1892, at 17 Arkinholm Terrace. His mother described him as "an eaten and spewed-up lookin' wee thing wi' een like twa burned holes in a blanket." His first winter was very severe. The Esk froze so solidly that horses and carts could travel up and down it for a distance of twenty miles, and young Chris, wrapped in a Shetland shawl, was taken to the door of the house to see the townsfolk skating on the river. His father was a rural postman whose route took him up the Ewes valley as far as Fiddleton Toll Bar, while his mother was caretaker at Langholm Library.

Young Chris was enrolled at Langholm Infant School (now the County Library and Day Centre) when he reached the age of five. Two years later he moved into the Primary Department of Langholm Academy. One of his teachers was a Hawick man, Francis George Scott, who as well as teaching general subjects was also music master. In later life the two men were re-united and Scott set seventy of Grieve's poems to music; in return the poet dedicated his epic poem *A Drunk Man Looks at the Thistle* to his mentor. As a boy Grieve would climb the stairs from the ground floor flat in the Library Buildings, where they now lived, to the Library above, carrying an empty washing basket which he would fill with books – his reading material for the week! In his autobiography, *Lucky Poet*, he said that he knew the library so well that "I could go up into that library in the dark and find any book I wanted … I can still remember not only whereabout on the shelves all sorts of books were, but whereabouts in the books themselves were favourite passages or portions that interested me specially for one reason or another".

Chris Grieve's father James was a kirk elder and the superintendent of the Langholm South United Free Church Sunday School. He held such strong Presbyterian views that he would not allow Robert Burns' poems to be read in the house, presumably because he objected to the way the poet satirised the hypocrisy of the Kirk in works like *Holy Willie's Prayer*.

When thirteen, Chris became a Sunday school teacher (a move which would clash violently with his philosophies in later life) and taught the tiny tots each Sunday. He also attended Bible Class each week at the home of Rev Cairncross. This local minister, a book reviewer for the *Irish Times*, was a poet in his own right and had an extensive library to which he gave Grieve free access.

In November 1908 a three-stanza poem called *Memories of Langholm* appeared in the local paper, the *Eskdale and Liddesdale Advertiser*. Written under the pseudonym Alister K Laidlaw, it was the first poem Grieve had published.

> 'How horrible the clatter and the noise
> That jars eternally!
> There is no music in the voice
> Of the city.
> But, Oh! The sweet sad song Ewes used to sing
> Is ringing in my ears.
> Its magic tingling still will ring
> Throughout the years.'

However, by the time it appeared in print he had left Langholm to enrol as a pupil teacher at Broughton Higher Grade School and Junior Student Centre, Edinburgh. George Ogilvie, the Principal English teacher, immediately spotted the boy's amazing potential and became a mentor and great friend to him.

He left Broughton in 1911, but rather than go into teaching as his father had hoped he would, he embarked on an entirely different career – as a newspaper journalist. His first job was as a freelance journalist at home in Langholm, but over the years Grieve was to work as a reporter and editor for many provincial newspapers throughout Scotland, England and Wales. Many of these jobs were quite short-lived. During the First World War he was made a Quarter Master Sergeant and then Sergeant in the 42nd General Hospital, RAMC in Salonica. Whilst abroad he contracted malaria, and was invalided home. It was at this time that he married his first wife, Peggy Skinner, who was secretary to the Colonel of the Black Watch at Queen's Barracks, Perth. When pronounced fit again he was posted to Sections Lahore Indian General Hospital near Marseilles in France, which dealt with the repatriation of mentally disturbed Asiatics. Mortality rates in the wards were high and Grieve's job was to organise the cremation of those who had died during the previous night. He was also in charge of the supplies of um and brandy, which were to be administered to the Sikhs for medical purposes. As the Sikhs were strictly teetotal, he was able to find alternative uses for the spirit!

When the war ended, he found temporary work cataloguing the book collection of Dyson Perrins, the Worcester Sauce millionaire, at Ardross Castle before becoming a reporter with the *Montrose Review* in 1919. He stayed with the paper for ten years and during that time settled down in Montrose as a Justice of the Peace and town councillor.

In August 1922 he wrote a piece of English prose for the first volume of *The Scottish Chapbook* entitled *Nisbet: An Interlude in Post-War Glasgow* under the name Hugh MacDiarmid, which was the first time he used his Celtic pseudonym.

Grieve joined PEN International, an international association of literary people, in 1923 and during meetings in London rubbed shoulders with such luminaries as George Bernard Shaw and H G Wells.

Chris Grieve believed passionately in Home Rule for Scotland and his poetry and politics were inextricably linked. As such, he was one of the founder members of the National Party of Scotland, which was formed in April 1928 to unify the various groups which were already advocating Home Rule. Six years later, this party amalgamated with the Scottish Party to become the Scottish National Party.

Grieve moved to the Shetland Island of Whalsay with his second wife Valda Trevlyn and their baby son, Michael in 1933. The family lived in dire poverty in this "self-induced Scottish Siberia", existing on a diet of mutton, mackerel, cod roe and vegetables, supplemented with gulls' eggs, which were collected and pickled for the winter. What little money they received came in the form of advances from publishers for the great amount of writing he did at that time. In 1934 he was one of a group who travelled to London intent on stealing the Stone of Destiny and returning it to Scotland. However, the tight security in the Abbey made the task impossible and they abandoned the operation.

Chris Grieve and his wife, Valda, at the Common Riding of 1978

During the Second World War, the family moved from Whalsay to Glasgow. Because Grieve had suffered a severe mental breakdown five years before this, he was pronounced unfit for heavy work. Instead, he was employed as a precision fitter in Mechan's Engineering Company, Glasgow, which specialised in producing war materials. He was transferred to the Merchant Service two years later, serving aboard the Norwegian vessel, "HMV Gurli" as first engineer.

In January 1951 the family was offered a run-down two-roomed cottage on the farm of Brownsbank, near Biggar. It had no electricity, running water nor inside toilet but it was "somewhere to live" and, more importantly, it had the advantage of being rent-free! Brownsbank was where Grieve spent the rest of his life. Valda soon set about making the cottage not only habitable but comfortable, and with the help of students from Edinburgh University, they gradually added electric light, a bathroom with flushing toilet and a kitchenette. Valda even lined an outhouse with orange boxes so that her husband would have somewhere to store all his papers and books.

In August 1971, while preparing to celebrate his seventy-ninth birthday, he was struck down with severe abdominal pain. It took four years to diagnose the problem, a severe, and by then inoperable, cancer of the large bowel. With his characteristic dogged determination he soldiered on valiantly to the end, even

The memorial in Langholm Cemetery

travelling to Dublin two months before his death to receive an honorary title of LittD from Trinity College.

On 9th September 1978 Christopher Murray Grieve died in Chalmers Hospital, Edinburgh – but the poet Hugh MacDiarmid still lives on in the psyche of the Scottish people.

Despite all the friction which existed, Grieve always maintained that Langholm "was the bonniest place he knew in the whole wide world" and that it had been his "touchstone in all creative matters". The strong emotional ties he had with his birthplace never weakened. On the 12th August 1972 a poem written by Valda appeared in *The Scotsman* to mark the poet's eightieth birthday.

> 'Over the years you've dreamed your dreams
> And as always
> You go back to your past
> In Langholm – your tap-root.'

It was his wish that he should be buried back home in the town. So on Wednesday 13th September 1978, the prodigal son finally returned home to his roots. Under a dreich, but typical border sky, several hundred friends and admirers huddled under umbrellas round his grave in Langholm Cemetery. As a piper played the pibroch, *Lament for the Children*, Valda placed "the little white roses of Scotland" on his coffin. His friend, the poet Norman MacCaig said that he had "walked into my mind as if it were a town and he a torchlight procession of one". He also suggested in a poem that MacDiarmid's passing would be marked by "two minutes of pandemonium!"

On the side of Whita Hill, where a memorial exists to another famous son of Eskdale, the Scottish Sculpture Trust and Scottish Arts Council erected a steel monument by Jake Harvey to his memory in 1985.

Hugh MacDiarmid was the single most influential figure in twentieth century Scots literature. The man, and his works, were complex and at times contradictory; but that was the way he liked it. Fuelled by his strong political views he could be vain in the extreme, as when he said, "I myself am Scotland today", but he could also be kind, charming and generous. He was never content to take the well-trodden path, always preferring to exist "whaur extremes meet". He set himself one task in life, to recreate the Scots language. He strove to reshape Scots as the living language of Scotland, much as the Norwegians had done with their language, to replace the parochialised Scots of Burns (who he said had reduced Scots writing to "a Kailyard") with a language that would better suit the "more complex requirements of our urban civilisation". The 'Synthetic Scots' that MacDiarmid created, known as Lallans, was based on the Scots border tongue, but also used Scots words from any region or period in its history. He created a language from a myriad of tongues, which was able to suggest meaning, even if the exact meaning of the words was not clear to the reader:

> 'Ae weet forenicht i' the yow-trummle
> I saw yon antrin thing,
> A watergaw wi' its chitterin' licht
> Ayont the on-ding;
> An' I thocht o' the last wild look ye gied
> Afore ye deed!

There was nae reek i' the laverock's hoose
That nicht – an' nane i' mine;
But I hae thocht o' that foolish licht
Ever sin' syne;
An' I think that mebbe at last I ken
What your look meant then.'

The Watergaw

MacDiarmid wrote over forty books of poetry and prose. His chief works are his three *Hymns to Lenin* and his long epic, *A Drunk Man Looks at the Thistle*, which found its inspiration in the imagery associated with that great border festival – Langholm Common Riding.

'Drums in the Walligate, pipes in the air,
Come and hear the cryin' o' the Fair.
A' as it used to be, when I was a loon
On Common-Ridin' Day in the Muckle Toon.

The bearer twirls the Bannock-and-Saut-Herrin',
The Croon o' Roses through the lift is farin',
The aught-fit thistle wallops on hie;
In heather besoms a' the hills gang by.'

Christopher Murray Grieve always courted controversy, but the glut of honours that were laid at his feet only strengthens the claim that he, single-handedly, brought about a renaissance in Scottish Literature.

14

The Moon-Man's Visit

At the Eskdale Burns' Club's Annual Supper in 1966, the Chief Guest, Mr James Finlayson from Hawick, expressed the hope "that a reconciliation might be effected between the author (MacDiarmid) and his birthplace, and that Langholm might not delay too long in honouring him". His remarks were greeted with cries of "Never, Never!" and "Git away back tae Hawick!" Langholm's most famous son never did receive the recognition he deserved from his native town. Instead, the honorary title of Freeman of the Burgh was conferred for the first and only time on an American descendant of the Armstrong Clan who had 'boldly gone where no man had gone before' – Commander Neil Alden Armstrong, the first man to set foot on the moon.

Saturday, 11th March 1972 will long be remembered as the date of the greatest civic ceremony this town has ever seen. The eyes of the world were fixed on Langholm that day, the day the town chose to honour a man of almost superhuman achievement.

Almost three years had passed since the world watched, awestruck, as the frail, spidery craft called "The Eagle" finally touched down on the silent, barren surface of the moon. The man who took those first tentative steps had, by his actions, fired the imaginations of countless millions and burned his name indelibly into the history books.

In 1970, an exiled Langholmite, the Rev Jimmy Beverley of Houston, Texas was asked by the Provost and Town Council to deliver a parcel of gifts to the astronaut at the Manned Spacecraft Centre in Houston. In a letter to the author, Jimmy Beverley explains "Jimmy Grieve asked us if it wad be a hardship tae bring a percel and hand it in at NASA. Of coorse, hevun a whole lot o' respect for the baking Provost I telt um it wad be nae bother at a'! Hei added, if ee git tae see um personally wad ee invite him tae cum tae Langholm". Rev Beverley, his two children and a friend duly met the great man and were bowled over by his warm sincerity, his humility and by the size of his inner sanctum, which was barely half the size of his own study at home! He had prepared a 'highfaluttin' speech extolling Langholm and the rich history of the area, but in the circumstances, all was forgotten. He was also impressed by the astronaut's knowledge of Armstrong folklore and history, as his vocabulary included local place names like Canonbie, Gilnockie and Carlenrig. When the subject of a possible visit was raised, he showed genuine interest and said that he would make every effort to visit Langholm whilst in Britain. The astronaut then took the party into the Public Relations Room at the Centre and graciously posed with Jimmy and his children while photographs were taken. Rev Beverley concluded, "When we left Mr Armstrong's office it was with the feeling of having been in the presence of greatness".

Sometime later, when it was known that Neil Armstrong, then a Professor of Engineering at Cincinnati University, would be coming to Scotland to propose the Mountbatten Lecture at Edinburgh University, it was unanimously agreed by the Town Council that he should be re-invited to visit his ancestral home and, if willing, accept the honorary title of Freeman of the Burgh.

On this great occasion the Town Council chose to ignore the old unrevoked statute, which states that any Armstrong who sets foot in Langholm will be hanged!

By the time Professor and Mrs Armstrong arrived in the town on that day in March 1972, fully half an hour behind schedule, the Market Place was packed with locals and visitors alike and with a heavy contingent of journalists and television crews from around the world. Under a cloudless sky the crowd fell silent as the Town Band struck up *The Star-Spangled Banner,* before erupting into loud cheers as *Scotland the Brave* was played.

After a short spell in the Town Hall, the official party, which included Provost and Mrs Grieve, was carried in great style to the Parish Kirk in the back of a beautiful landau pulled by two flighty greys, flanked by two Halberdiers and led by the stirring strains of Langholm Pipe Band. The congregation of 1,500 souls rose as one, to accord the moon-man a momentous welcome as he walked down the aisle to the strains of *See the Conquering Hero Comes,* played out on the mighty Parish Kirk organ. After Provost Grieve formally welcomed the astronaut, the Town Clerk, Eddie Armstrong was called upon to read aloud the Burgess Ticket: -

> *AT LANGHOLM on the Eleventh day of March, Nineteen-Hundred-and-Seventy-two.* **WHICH DAY the PROVOST, MAGISTRATES and COUNCILLORS of the BURGH of LANGHOLM** *in pursuance of a Resolution unanimously adopted at a Special Meeting of the Council held on the Eleventh day of August Nineteen hundred and sixty nine admitted and received as they do hereby admit and receive*
>
> **NEIL ALDEN ARMSTRONG**
>
> *to be a Burgess and Freeman of the Burgh of Langholm with all the rights, privileges and immunities thereto belonging, in recognition of his outstanding achievements in the exploration of space, and of the skill and leadership shown by him when as Commander of the Apollo XI Lunar Expedition, he became the first man to set foot on the moon, taking mankind's first step onto another planet.*
>
> Extracted from the Records of the Town Council
Edward C Armstrong, Town Clerk

Provost Grieve then went on to say, "My friends, the man who manoeuvred that safe and gentle landing on the moon, the man at the controls, sits beside me. It is his skill, courage and his superior qualities of leadership we recognise today, for he above all epitomises the mighty achievements of man in space. This man from Wapakonets is an Armstrong, and is immediately descended from the Irish branch of the family. That simple fact establishes the link with Langholm and Eskdale, for history records that the Armstrongs of Gilnockie and the 'Muckle Toon' founded this branch. This is Armstrong country, and has been for centuries, and it is hardly surprising there was no hesitation in inviting you, Professor Armstrong, to become our first Freeman".

Professor Armstrong taking the Oath of Allegiance to Langholm in the Parish Church

Professor Armstrong was then called upon to take the Oath of Allegiance to Langholm and then to sign the Minute Book. Having done this, Provost Grieve then formally admitted Professor Armstrong as a Freeman and Honorary Burgess of the Burgh of Langholm. He was then presented with his Burgess Ticket, which was made from the finest calf vellum and embossed with the Burgh Coat of Arms. It was contained in the Burgess Casket, made from seasoned walnut, and which was a replica of Johnnie Armstrong's stronghold at Gilnockie.

Professor Armstrong received a standing ovation as he addressed the assembly, "It is said that the most difficult place to be recognised is in one's home town – I consider Langholm to be my home town. Langholm people are my kind of people. And while this is my first trip to Langholm, I hope it will not be my last".

The ceremony came to an unforgettable end as the congregation sang *The 23rd Psalm* to the tune *Crimond*, before the new Burgess, together with the Provost and members of the Town Council, left the church to attend a formal luncheon held in the Buccleuch Hall.

Provost Grieve again presided over the proceedings, which were attended by the Provosts and Mayors of no fewer than nine neighbouring Border Towns as well as their Graces, The Duke and Duchess of Buccleuch. The Provost again spoke of Professor Armstrong's career as a fighter pilot during the Korean War and then as a test pilot and astronaut. When he pledged a toast to Langholm's first Freeman, the company rose again to give the astronaut a standing ovation. Miss Jean White, the Treasurer of the Town Council, then presented the couple with a series of gifts – lengths of cloth from each of the mills and drapers in the Town. Professor Armstrong's companions on his intrepid journey to the moon were not forgotten either, as gifts were also given to him to pass on to Col Edwin E Aldrin and Col Michael Collins.

On his return to America, Professor Armstrong sent a photograph of himself on the moon, taken by "Buzz" Aldrin, as a gift to the people of Langholm. It now hangs proudly in the Council Chamber in Langholm Town Hall.

A brass plaque on the wall of the Langholm Parish Kirk commemorates the occasion. It is sited in an area of the church that was originally reserved for the sole use of the Buccleuch family. It now provides a haven for those children whose imaginations carry them far beyond the realms of the minister's sermons!

Meeting the people outside the Buccleuch Hall

The astronaut and his wife left Langholm in the mid-afternoon en route to Drumlanrig Castle, where they spent the night as guests of the Duke and Duchess of Buccleuch. The party stopped at Gilnockie Tower, just south of Langholm, where they met Sir Fergus Graham of Netherby before completing the journey flanked by a police escort.

In the space of a few short hours Langholm witnessed a visit from one of the greatest living icons of the twentieth century. No-one present that day will ever forget the quiet, unassuming man who by taking "one small step for man" had rewritten the history books forever.

Professor Armstrong vowed he would return to Langholm one day, but only on his own terms, which were that he be treated like any other anonymous visitor to the town. Although his mother and brother have since visited, he has not yet kept his promise. Let us hope that that day dawns soon.

> 'Will ye no come back again?
> Will ye no come back again?
> Better lo'ed ye canna be,
> Will ye no come back again?'
>
> Lady Nairne

15

❧ Langholm Rugby Fitba' Club ❧

Half a mile north of the town, near the hill road to Newcastleton, lies the hallowed turf of Milntown – the home of Langholm Rugby Football Club. This local institution is home to one of the most feared groups in the whole of Scottish Rugby – 'The Langholm Waterside Crowd', with their war cry "Dig a hooel Langholm and bury tha b***ers."

When you consider the club's lack-lustre record over the past few decades, many find it difficult to believe that Langholm was the Club which introduced Rugby Football to the Scottish Borders.

The origins of the game go back centuries, long before the famous incident at Rugby School, when William Webb Ellis picked up a football and ran with it. Indeed there is a tradition of 'the handling game' in the Scottish Borders, which can be traced back to Roman times, when the soldiers played a game called 'Harpastum'. The custom of Ba' or Handba', which has carried on in the Borders for centuries, was and still is played between the 'Uppies' and 'Doonies' of various Border towns much to the consternation of the shopkeepers and general population alike.

In December 1815 a bizarre game of Ba' was organised at Carterhaugh near Bowhill by Charles, Duke of Buccleuch, and Sir Walter Scott. The Earl of Home (the Duke's Brother-in-law) captained a side made up of estate tenants from the Ettrick and Yarrow valleys, while the other team was composed of townsmen from Selkirk, augmented with contingents from Galashiels and Hawick. With several hundred players on each side and with the goals (marked off stretches of the rivers Yarrow and Ettrick) almost a mile part, it was sport on a massive scale. Before play started, Scott's son, also called Walter, paraded the ancient banner of the Scotts of Buccleuch before the teams. It was reckoned that this was the first time this hallowed relic had been seen in public since the funeral of Earl Walter in 1633.

The Duke started the game by throwing the ball into the air before beating a hasty retreat to avoid being trampled as the two sides collided in a massive scrum. By half time it was evident that things were not going the Scotts' way as they were losing by one hail (goal) to nil; so Sir Walter was dispatched to the Galashiels contingent to persuade them to break ranks and defect to the other side. This they did, and soon an Ettrick man equalised the score by winning a hail in the Yarrow. The game had to be stopped after five hours when dusk began to fall. The Selkirk men were furious at this deceit, and set out to wreak vengeance on the Galashiels men. Those unfortunate enough to be separated from the main pack were pounced on and severely 'hemmert'. It has been suggested that this shameful episode triggered the now familiar cry of "Dirty Gala"!

There is evidence that by the early 1820s some kind of handling game was being played by the pupils at the High School of Edinburgh.

By 1871 rugby was being played within the narrow confines of schools in Edinburgh and Glasgow, with teams like Edinburgh Wanderers and West of Scotland being formed to accommodate the overflow from the schools' FPs sides. But there was no organised rugby in the Borders until Old Year's Day 1871, when the sons of three wealthy Langholm mill owners, William Scott, Alf Moses and William Lightbody, invited the young men of the town to the Lamb Hill to try the new fangled game of rugby. The three had been introduced to the game at private school and were keen to promote it in Langholm. The notion of forming a rugby club in the town first came to them as they kicked a ball about the field at Lightbody's tweed mill, in the winter of 1871. In his excellent booklet, *Langholm's First Hundred*, Walter Bell maps out the first hundred years of the Club. The most inspirational figure during these very early days was William Scott, co-founder of Criterion Mills. Because of his leadership qualities, he became the first captain, president, secretary and treasurer of this new Club, which was formed in the first weeks of 1872, following a meeting held in the Buccleuch Hotel. As the sole authority on the rules of the game, William Scott's word was law, and any player who upset him during the week "wadna be picked for the team on Seterday"!

In the 1872-73 season the Duke of Buccleuch allowed Langholm RFC the use of the Castleholm for the nominal rent of one shilling a year. They remained there until the Duke offered them their current home at Milntown (Scotsholm) in October 1898. The Duke not only flattened the ground but also built a bridge across the river Ewes to improve access. The players' kit in those early days was practically non-existent. The local lads did not have the resources to buy proper rugby boots, so they were forced to improvise by nailing strips of leather (from surplus drive belts from the mills) to the soles of their boots. Langholm's first rugby ball was hand-made by a local saddler.

The earliest 'battles' were fought out between the Old and New Town, but soon games were being played at Canonbie and Westerkirk and fixtures were being arranged with teams from further afield, such as Waterbeck and Springkell. The games with the Canonbie Club, which was founded by the local minister, Rev Dr Barclay in 1875, would often degenerate into 'punch-ups' as few knew the rules. Hacking was quite common during these early games and players could trip up an opponent without violating the rules. During one game, a Canonbie player was sent off for biting a Langholm player in the 'nether regions' during a scrum!

To improve the players' knowledge of the game, a copy of the Rugby rules was obtained from the *Yorkshire Post* and they were encouraged to learn, and put into practice, ten rules each week.

Another piece of rugby history was made on 23rd March 1873, when Langholm played Carlisle for the first time. Over the years this has become the oldest fixture in the world between two club teams from different countries, and now takes place on or near every New Year's Day. The first game was played on the Castle Holm at Langholm, and had been preceded by a trial match the week before, between the Old and New Town. Unfortunately, the occasion was marred by a great deal of controversy, the main bones of contention were whether the ball should be kicked over or under the bar to win a goal and the number of players in each team. Carlisle insisted on having 25 men per side, whereas Langholm argued that it should be only 20. In the end, William Scott lost patience and 'laid down the law', as it was Langholm's pitch and Langholm's ba'! The first 'cross-border skirmish' since the reiving days, ended in a victory for Langholm by two goals to nil, but had to be abandoned when it became too dark to see the ball.

The first match between Langholm and their great rivals, Hawick was played at Hawick on 31st January 1874. Hawick and Wilton Cricket Club had founded the Hawick Club in 1873, and this match with Langholm was the first full match they ever played. Langholm offered to bring their ball if Hawick did not possess one, and insisted on playing under their rules. During these early days, the goals at the Hawick ground were little more than two sticks with a piece of tape tied between them. The game ended in a no-score draw and was, by all accounts, contentious. It should be explained that in those days a referee was felt unnecessary; the rival captains acted as adjudicators in all disputes. A thrang (argumentative) captain like William Scott could cause long and acrimonious hold-ups.

By the mid 1880s there were two other teams in Langholm. The 'Bullfield Team' played on the field adjoining Holmfoot at the south end of the town, while the 'West End' team played on the land that was later taken up by John Young's transport business and is now owned by G J Latimer & Co. There was fierce competition amongst the three local teams; the order of merit was usually the Langholm team followed by the Bullfield team with the West End team bringing up the rear. The Bullfield Club were fortunate in having Geordie Duncan, the celebrated Powderhall sprinter, as one of their key players; he was regarded as being one of the finest halfs in the South of Scotland at the time. Another exceptional player was J McVittie, said to have been one of the finest forwards ever to have graced the rugby field. He eventually left Langholm and went to Manchester where he joined the Salford Club, who were joint champions of England along with Bradford. He also played for Lancashire, and would certainly have played for England if he had been eligible to do so. Although he played against some of the best teams in England and Wales, he thought highly of his native team and maintained that "in certain respects the Langholm Club could not be excelled".

J Scott was the most consistent scorer the Club possessed and rarely played without scoring at least once. Scott received his training at Craigmount School in Edinburgh and, showing exceptional ability, was drawn into the Edinburgh Wanderers team. He captained the South of Scotland side on several occasions during the 1880s, but owing to the fact that he was relatively unknown, only made it onto the reserves bench of the national team, and did not receive the Cap that so many thought he richly deserved.

By the beginning of the 1890s Langholm, along with their great rivals Hawick, were two of the most powerful sides in the country. One fan was so carried away by the team's success that he composed a little ditty entitled *Oor Fitba Team* which was sung to the tune *A man's A man for aw that*.

> 'Oor Fitba' lads are fleet an' fit,
> Baith stoot an' strang an' aw that
> In front the goal they aye can get,
> Score ties an' goals like aw that

For aw that an' aw that
Through wun an' rain an' aw that
They force the game an' raise oor fame
Mid cheering lood an' aw that.

It was a gran and glorious sicht,
We saw that day an' aw that
When Eskdale's sons in aw their micht
Ower turned the Greens an' aw that
For aw that and aw that
They late became an' aw that
They left like fish amang the brine
Gay soor, an' salt and aw that.'

Langholm Cronie, November 1891

1892 saw a fresh face appearing in the ranks of the Langholm team. Young Tom Scott who was another member of the tweed mill dynasty, and had just returned home from private school in Edinburgh to take up a position in the family firm. His great skill on the field did not go unnoticed. By 1895 he had been chosen to represent the South of Scotland. Later in the same season he received the supreme accolade when he received the first of his eleven Caps, against Wales. It was doubly fitting that he should be chosen to play that year, as this was the semi-jubilee of the Club's formation. In the game against Ireland in 1898 (which became known as "The Tom Scott Match") his two tries earned Scotland a victory in Belfast by a goal and a try, to nil. When he hung up his boots, Scott, the greatest three quarterback the game has ever produced, became President of the Langholm Club before going on to become the first

Tom Scott with his wife, Ethel,
and sons, Alex and baby William Sutton

Borderer to be appointed President of the Scottish Rugby Union in 1914. At the tender age of thirty-eight he was also the youngest man ever to hold that title.

During the 1901-02 season 'the Big Seven' – Langholm, Hawick, Galashiels, Melrose, Jed-Forest and later Kelso and Selkirk – decided that the occasional fixtures that were played amongst the border teams each season were wholly inadequate and so it was decided that a local league should be formed to promote hot-blooded competition amongst the various border sides. The Border League, the oldest Rugby Union league in the world, was formed in a back room of the King's Arms Hotel in Melrose by these teams, much to the displeasure of the Scottish Rugby Union, which failed to recognise it for seventy-two years. Those usurpers keen to remove the present day Langholm RFC from The Border League would do well to bear in mind the major part this Club played in the league's formation over one hundred years ago.

By the early 1920s the team's fortunes were on the wane as they began to run short of promising young players. The appearance of a talented young fourteen year old must have set their spirits soaring. John Goodfellow was immediately drafted into the first fifteen and played alongside his fullback father, J V Goodfellow (a gifted sevens player) and a cousin, also called John Goodfellow. In February 1928 Goodfellow became Langholm's second internationalist, when as a reserve against Wales at Murrayfield he was brought into the game to replace I S Smith. He subsequently won two other Caps that season against Ireland and England.

It would be another twenty-two years before Langholm folk would recognise a 'kent face' in the national team. Donald Scott was one of the young protégés of the Rev J L Cotter, local minister and ex-internationalist, during the post war revival of rugby in the town. He played the central role in Langholm's spectacular 5-0 victory over Melrose in the final of Selkirk Sevens in 1949. His single try in that final rocked the foundations of Border rugby, and heralded the dawn of the greatest decade in the Club's long history. By rights Donald Scott should have received his first Cap that season but National Service put paid to that. Instead he had to wait until February the following year to receive the first of his ten Caps, playing on the right wing in the match against Ireland in Dublin. Although Scotland was soundly beaten by 21 points to nil, the Langholm man brought the crowd to its feet on several occasions with some thrilling clearances and tackles.

Even if Langholm could produce a formidable seven at this time, it took until the 1954-55 season before the first fifteen got their game back on track. The season started brilliantly when the Club won Earlston Sevens, defeating Hawick in the final. The headlines in the *Sunday Post* next day announced, "A New Star is Born". It referred to Tony Grieve's debut in a final, when he made two spectacular tries which won Langholm the Sevens. The South Selectors were beginning to show interest in some of the young talent that Langholm had to offer, so much so that in October that year no fewer than four Langholm players, J Maxwell, C Elliot, J Telford and T Grieve, were in the South team that beat Glasgow 18-11, contributing 14 of the 18 points won.

The following season got off with a bang when Langholm won Gala Sevens for only the second time, beating the home team in the final. In 1957 Jimmy Maxwell finally received the recognition he deserved when he was picked to play stand-off against Ireland at Murrayfield in the midst of a blinding snowstorm. Jimmy's moment of glory was short-lived, for he was cruelly switched only ten minutes into the game and was never given the opportunity to represent his country again. However, he remained a potent force in club and border rugby and went on to captain the team in their 'hour of glory'.

The next year saw another Langholm name written into the annals of Scottish Rugby's hall of fame. For in March 1958 Langholm winger Christie Elliot made his debut for Scotland in the Calcutta Cup match against the 'auld enemy', England, at Murrayfield. Although ending in only a draw it was a thrilling match. Elliot, who replaced the Scottish captain Arthur Smith laid low with flu, certainly impressed the 60,000 spectators with his strong running, determined tackling and his goal kicking reputation which he proved by kicking a penalty ten minutes into the second half. Christie went on to win another 11 national Caps and the reputation of being one of the finest wingers the Scottish Borders has ever produced. In the 1957-58 season he set a Club and national record for that time by scoring 270 points. In a game against Allan Glens FP he amassed an amazing 35 points by scoring four tries, kicking ten conversions and one penalty.

However, greater glory was to follow in the 1958-59 season when Langholm swept all before them. Not only were they unofficial Scottish and Border League Champions, but they also won Langholm Sevens and were undefeated in every game they played – even against the mighty London Scottish. By the end of that season Langholm was the only team out of 420 British teams listed in the *Sunday Times* to remain unbeaten. At the end of the season Langholm headed the Scottish Championship table with a percentage of 89, having played 19 games in which they won 15, drew 4 and lost none. The crucial game of the season took place at The Greenyards and on that April night 'all roads from Langholm led to Melrose'. In front of a crowd of 3,500 Christie Elliot kicked three fine penalties against two unconverted tries by Melrose's "Moose" Hastie and Andrew Hewat. In desperation, Hastie went for a drop goal in the final minutes of the game … but it was not to be. Amid scenes of unbridled jubilation, the Langholm supporters stormed the pitch and carried the players shoulder-high to the pavilion to receive the Border League cup from their President and teammate, Hector Monro, who was also Chairman of the Border League.

When the triumphant team returned home that night, they were met by the Pipe Band at the Townhead Tollbar and were carried shoulder high down the High Street to the Town Hall, to be officially congratulated by Provost Hyslop, who toasted their continuing success in champagne drunk out of the Border League Cup. When the Town Band struck up with Handel's *See the Conquering Hero Comes* (which ironically had been written to celebrate a different victory two hundred years before – the return of the 'Butcher of Cumberland' to London, after Culloden) the crowd of 1,500 went berserk and the clapping and cheering was deafening. Two brave souls climbed on to the roof of the Town Hall and hoisted the Langholm club's flag up the flagpole, where it remained for several days. Provost Hyslop was not the first to fill the cup; it had been filled at several places on the way home. In the town a second magnum of champagne was provided by Mr Mercer of the Eskdale Hotel and a third by Mr Lunn of the Ashley Bank Hotel. In Hawick a woman had also thrust a bottle of whisky into the hands of a local supporter as they travelled home to Langholm by car. It was stipulated that it be

Jimmy Maxwell receiving the Border League cup from Hector Monro

used "tae fill the cup" – and it was. When the Band rounded off that memorable evening with *Craigielea* and *Auld Lang Syne*, few present did not feel a lump come to their throat or a tear well up in their eye.

That was the sweetest moment in the Langholm Club's long history; they have never equalled it.

The Club held a celebration dinner in June of that year, when the following poem was read out.

> 'There's a wee toon on the Borders,
> Renowned for Rugby fame;
> The greatest team in Scotland,
> Langholm is its name.
>
> They've won the Scottish Championship,
> The Border League an' aw;
> Unbeaten and unsullied,
> Their heids aboon them aw.
>
> The Sevens season started,
> The City teams all thought
> They could come to the Borders
> And try to win the lot.

But when they came to Langholm,
On Milntown's lovely green,
The TV cameras all were there,
And history was "seen".

Out came the Bhoys in crimson;
The other ties were tame,
They showed the Edinburgh teams
Just how to play the game.

Christie, Jimmy, Tony, Bill,
Two Andys, Sandy too,
The greatest Langholm Seven
Since eighteen seventy-two.

The final tie was grand to see,
The Bhoys turned on the power;
The opposition never scored,
'Twas 'Langholm's Finest Hour'.

Long live the Langholm Rugby Club,
Long live the Bhoys an' a',
Let's hope in nineteen sixty
They'll still be "on the ba'".'

Anon

The winning team at the 1959 Langholm Sevens
l – r back row: Billy Murray, Christie Elliot, Tony Grieve, Andrew Jeffrey
front row: Zander Turnbull, Jimmy Maxwell, Andy Warwick

Nineteen sixty-eight was to see a second young star from the Elliot stables win national acclaim. Tommy Elliot, Christie's younger brother, made local history by becoming the first local forward to be capped for his country in the match against Wales at Cardiff Arms Park. Unfortunately, Tommy injured his knee during the game, leaving him unfit to play in the Irish match later that season, despite going through all the preliminary training sessions. However, Tommy went on to play another four times for his country. At regional level he was chosen, along with teammate Irving Davidson, to play in the Scottish Borders team that toured South Africa in 1967. Both he and his Vice-Captain, Neil Stevenson, played in that thrilling match between The South and the South Africans at Galashiels in January 1970.

The early 1960s saw the emergence of a new generation of players thanks largely to the efforts of Jim Tuton, the Academy's PE teacher. The recently formed Colts side was an excellent environment in which to nurture this raw young talent.

One young star to emerge from the chrysalis of school rugby was William (Billy) Steele. Billy was already in the RAF when chosen, without a trial, to represent his country in the match against England at Twickenham in 1969. At the end of that season he was picked to be part of the Scottish team which toured Argentina. Billy played for his country no fewer than twenty-three times, earning him the title 'Langholm's most capped man'. He was selected for the British Lions tour of South Africa in 1974, and had the distinction of playing in the first two Test Matches against the Springboks. As the 'choirmaster' during that tour, he is also credited with introducing the song *Flower of Scotland* into Scottish Rugby culture. Billy also played regularly for the Barbarians, and was one of the seven which competed at Langholm Sevens during the Centenary year. He never abandoned his roots, and whenever possible would return home to play for his 'auld team', particularly in the Sevens.

Stephen Turk is the only other local player to have climbed up through the ranks from school to national rugby. In the 1968-69 season Turk exceeded Christie Elliot's scoring record for a single season by an amazing 78 points (348 points). As skipper, during the 1970-71 season, Turk led the team to victory in its first twelve games. During the match with Langholm's great rivals, Hawick, that season he contributed to the 6-0 win with a penalty. Then late on in the second half, Christie Elliot scored the only try of the match. The crowd at Mansfield rose as one to afford him a standing ovation, this being the 22nd year to the day since he first pulled on the scarlet jersey of Langholm. In March 1971, a few minutes into the game, Turk ran onto the Twickenham turf to join his 'auld freen' and team mate, Billy Steele, in facing a formidable foe. This marked the first and only time that two Langholm men have played together in a national team.

However, there have been many others who have played a vital role in the Club's continuance over the years. Whether on the field or off it, they have worked tirelessly throughout the long periods of mediocrity to ensure that there is a future for Langholm Rugby Football Club. It would be entirely wrong to mention any without mentioning all, but the fact that Langholm Rugby Football Club still exists 133 years after its inception is a glowing testament to them all.

While it is over thirty years since Langholm last produced a male internationalist, new homespun talent is still emerging from the ranks. This is evident from the number of local young men who have been selected to play in the Scottish youth teams; to date, six local lads have been selected to play in under-18 teams for Scotland, two in under-19, and four for the under-21s.

In mentioning the young talent of recent years, Langholm's two lady internationalists must not be overlooked. Alison Little developed her skills as a nine year-old playing in the local Mini and Midi teams. She graduated to the Langholm Ladies' team, which had been formed to play in a Ladies' Sevens Tournament at a fun day at Melrose Rugby Club in 1984. While at John Moore's University in Liverpool, she played for their Ladies' team and received the first of her six Caps for Scotland Ladies' playing against Spain in the Ladies' Five Nations Championship in February 2000. Alison also played for Scotland in the European Championship in Spain in May 2000 and currently plays for the Waterloo Ladies' Team in Liverpool. Jilly McCord also developed her passion for the game while playing for the Langholm Ladies' team. She then went on to play for Edinburgh University Ladies' team from 1995 to 1999, and now plays for Watsonians Ladies' team in Edinburgh. In February 2004 Jilly was selected to play for Scotland in The Ladies' Six Nations Championship in Santiago de Compostela in Spain, although on this occasion only making it to the reserves' bench. However, in April/May of that year, she was selected to play in the Ladies' European Championship at Toulouse in France, receiving her first Cap playing in the matches against Sweden and France.

As already mentioned, the Langholm Club can boast of having a very healthy Mini/Midi Rugby training regime. In 2003 on average forty young boys of primary school age turned up each Sunday morning to train for the various mini teams; while around twenty-five boys of secondary school age train at the same time for the Midi teams. These teams compete in "friendlies" and in tournaments with teams from other border towns and can hold their own against any. If these young boys can be encouraged to stay with local rugby as they progress through school and into employment, then this will surely bode well for the future of the Club.

Sadly, money has blighted the modern game, for it now seems to be the main motivating force for many. All too often it has replaced the best quality a player can offer his team – loyalty. And yet so many disparities exist in respect to opportunities, facilities and coaching that it is impossible to blame those talented young players who have found it necessary to leave Milntown to develop their skills elsewhere.

In 2004 Langholm's first team is languishing in the Second Division of the National Leagues. It is probably true to say that it has been relegated into little more than a 'feeder team', supplying teams with fatter wallets with the talented young players who emerge from time to time. The halcyon days of the 1958-59 season are now but a memory, yet no one should ever underestimate the lads from Milntown, because every now and again, when least expected, a flash of genius will shine through.

This Club is looked upon with genuine warmth and respect by all other teams in the Scottish Union. It was very apt that, when talking about Border Rugby in his book, *The Borders*, Alistair Moffat chose the Langholm Club before all others.

Perhaps the momentous cheer, which rang out from The Greenyards on that April night in 1959, has never quite died away.

16

Langholm's Great Day

The Common Riding

'I'd rise wi' the rest on that lang-looked-for morning,
And clim' Whita's side wi' the heather see gay,
Tae see the bricht sun a' the valley adorning,
And rolling the mists like a curtain away.

I'd hear "A' the Airts" wake the hills that surroun' me,
And "The Flo'ers o' the Forest" sae plaintive and wae,
That tells o' the friens' wha oft gethered aroon' me,
But wha tae their faithers are noo passed away.

I'll hear, when the evening descends o'er the valley,
The he'rt-stirring strains o' the evergreen tune,
And see the gay throng roon the proud Cornet rally
And sing as they bring him again tae the toon.

What thoughts rise and fa' wi' the Ban' and the singing,
They gar mi auld he'rt fairly flutter wi' joy,
That tune, "Auld Lang Syne", oh, sae vividly bringing,
Tae min' a' the days I spent there when a boy.'

Where the Heather is Blowing,
An old Langholmite's Longing, by 'A T Wauchope'

No book about Langholm would be complete without mentioning a tradition which occupies a very special place in the hearts of many. The Common Riding is the embodiment of the town's communal pride, the jewel in its crown and the measure of its year. The Common Riding is the annual re-assertion of the town's identity, and the one day in the year when Langholm folk refuse to recognise any sovereignty – 'SAVE THIR AIN!'

To MacDiarmid, Langholm on Common Riding day was "warld enough" and there are many scattered throughout the globe, who will turn a tear-stained eye homeward and relive in their mind's eye the Common Ridings of yore.

There are four true Border Common Ridings. The Royal and Ancient Burgh of Lauder has the distinction of having the oldest and simplest. Of the other three, Selkirk is renowned for its Casting Ceremony and marvellous ride up the Lingley Burn to the Three Brethren and back; Hawick is renowned for its veritable glut of wonderful songs and music which make the rafters of 'The Hut' ring on Common Riding morning, but Langholm Common Riding is renowned for its TRADITION.

This tradition, which was borne out of necessity rather than design, is jealously guarded and arose from that most basic of all human rights – the right to belong.

For the last thousand years men from this valley have fought to retain what was theirs. Whenever the beacons blazed on the Border, these men have risen up 'in defence o' thir property' and have ridden off to fight with valour and distinction at Arkinholm, Flodden or more recently at Passchendale, the Somme or on the beaches of Normandy. Some found their last resting place at the bottom of a bog with a broadsword through their gut, while others lie on 'a foreign field', but all fought and some fell for the right to retain what was theirs.

The Marches are proudly ridden each year, not merely to guard a strip of boggy ground on the side of a hill from encroachment, but rather to protect a glorious heritage. It is this heritage, coupled with a real sense of community, which singles out Langholm from the thousands of soulless towns and cities dotted across Britain. The feelings of kinship are never stronger than on the last Friday in July when the oldest and youngest join in music, song and deed to celebrate a common identity.

The Common Riding of 1894

The Common Riding is a marriage of two unrelated events, which, over the centuries, have merged into the great people's festival that it is today. The older part was the Simmer or Lamb Fair, the largest Fair of its kind in the south of Scotland. It came into being in 1672, when the first Duke and Duchess of Buccleuch and Monmouth petitioned Parliament, to be allowed to hold two extra

Fairs in addition to those awarded to them in the Charter of 1621. One was on the 5th of April and the other, the Simmer Fair, was on the 15th day of July – 'auld style'. When Britain adopted the Gregorian calendar in 1752, the inherent error of eleven days was lost, meaning that the Fair now fell eleven days later, on the 26th day of July 'new style'. Although principally for the sale of lambs, sheep and wool, it also helped to foster local trade by allowing folk the opportunity to sell or barter other produce such as cheese, butter, flour, meal etc.

In his reminiscences of life over two hundred years ago, Walter Miller stated "the Simmer or Lamb Fair was held on the Kilngreen, Walker's Hole, the braes on the sides, and the Castle Green all the way up to the Milntown on the other side of the Ewes. The lambs sold for one shilling to three shillings a head, with the Potholm lambs generally getting the best price". It should be remembered that at this time the current road north by way of Walker's Hole and the Tourneyholm did not exist, and the Bar Wood had yet to be planted with trees. The lush land that made up the Miller's Hill (Lamb Hill) would slope unimpeded right down to the edge of the river. At Fair time this land, together with the Kilngreen and much of the Castle Hill, would literally be covered with lambs. For several days beforehand all roads leading into the town would be choked with great droves of lambs being piloted toward the hill by their plaided shepherds and faithful collie dogs. Miller could also remember how Hawick gardeners would attend the Fair with loads of berries in creels, which were carried on horseback. As a measure, they used a little wooden can, which had a false bottom, and they would cry, "Wha'll buy my cherry ripe greasels, spoutin' and birstin', twa fu's and a clert o'er for a bawbee or Scotch hapenny".

It is recorded that at the Simmer Fair of 1870 only one thousand lambs were "exposed for sale on the hill". Meanwhile in the Market Place there were twelve cart-loads of well-nourished 'grunters' (pigs), which sold at prices ranging from 20/- to 26/-. The report also mentions various colourful vendors who had stalls on the streets, such as the 'Sweety Wives' and the familiar strolling ballad singers. Both added an air to the proceedings, which was reminiscent of a much earlier time.

The Fair was also a day of reckoning, when accounts were settled and commitments were made for the incoming year. It was, to quote one source, the day when "the farmer bought his scythe and hay rake, and the wife her new bonnet and every servant lass received her 'fairing' (presents from the Fair) in ribbons, gingerbread and mint drops". The local hostelries were full to overflowing, and often the night between the Simmer Fair and Common Riding was spent in revelry, dancing, drinking – and fighting! This fact was highlighted by an incident, which allegedly happened just before the Simmer Fair of 1815, and involved the war-stained Scots Greys Regiment, which had just returned home after the great victory at Waterloo. The soldiers had ridden back into Scotland that day and had camped on the Kilngreen overnight.

Jane Rigg, a local woman who lived to the ripe old age of 102, could remember the excitement as they passed through the town, "all the town turned out, and many a Langholm eye ran wet at the sight of a mere handful of ragged and worn-out men – the relic of a whole regiment of braw, braw, lads."

The soldiers would be keen, no doubt, to celebrate their return to native soil with a prolonged spell of drinking in the local taverns. However, the Commanding Officer could see the danger in letting his men get mixed up with locals at the Fair next day, so at three o'clock in the morning they were rallied and made to ride north up the Chapel Path and out of danger.

The various local accounts of this incident contradict each other with regard to the year the Scots Greys returned to Scotland. Some claim that they returned in 1815, only five weeks after the battle, while others claim that they returned a year later, in 1816. However, in Edward Almack's book, *The History of the Second Dragoons (Royal Scots Greys)* which is regarded as the definitive account of this regiment's history, we are told that the Second Dragoons (Scots Greys) arrived back in England on January 12th 1817, before joining the depot at Canterbury two days later. In June of 1817, they marched north from Canterbury, presumably crossing the border on the day before the Simmer Fair that year. This claim is backed up by an article, which appeared in the *Carlisle Patriot* of 26th July 1817. It relates how "two squadrons of that fine Waterloo Regiment, the Scots Greys, passed through Carlisle this week on their way to Scotland".

While violence was common at the Fair, it was naïve to think that you were free of it once you left the town. In an edition of the *Carlisle Patriot,* dated August 1816, a gent, who wrote under the name Veritas, complained that people were regularly assaulted on the outskirts of Longtown, as they returned home from the Langholm Fair. It seems that it was common to be set upon by a pack of twenty to thirty local youths, who would bombard travellers with stones and clods of earth. He hoped that Sir James Graham of Netherby Hall would intervene and put an end to this "disgraceful and criminal conduct".

The Act of Parliament of 1672 gave the Baron, in this case the Duke of Buccleuch and Monmouth, the right to collect tolls and duties on all livestock and produce brought to the Simmer Fair. The Baron's representative in the town, the Baron Bailie, was responsible for collecting these tolls and duties and for the letting of all sites for stalls, although he would invariably hand this task to his deputy, the Baron Officer. However, before any of this could be legally enforced the Proclamation of the Fair had to be made – that is the Fair had to be 'cried' from the steps of the Mercat Cross.

The first man to proclaim the air was Jamie Ferguson, Bailie to the Laird of Ralton (probably William Elliot of Roan or Ralton in Liddesdale), who was Factor to the Duke. Ferguson lived within the Common Lands of Langholm near Middlemoss Farm.

Today the Fair (or Second Fair as it is commonly known) is cried firstly at the Castle Craigs by the Castle Craigs Fair Crier, before being cried again in the town square by the Fair Crier. It is a corruption of an older proclamation, which preceded 1672 (the year when the Simmer Fair came into existence) and is thought to refer to one of the two Fairs originally granted in the Nithsdale Charter of 1621. The text of "the fair" first appeared in print in the *Gentleman's Magazine* of 1731, and it was deemed "an old proclamation" even in those early times. Over the centuries the contents have changed and become anglicised as each subsequent Fair Crier has added his own flourishes and touches.

The Fair that was cried in Walter Miller's day was as follows: -

> 'Hoys Yes, that is ae time,
> Hoys Yes, again, that is twa times,
> Hoys Yes, that is the third and last time

This is to give notice, that there is a Muckle Fair to be hadden in the Muckle Toon o' Langholm on the 15th day of July auld style, upon His Grace the Duke of Buccleuch's merkland, for the space of eight days and upward; and a' land-loupers, and dub-skeppers and bell-the-gate swingers, and sturdy beggars that come here to bred any whordoms or dordordums, bulaments or tooliements, or to molest or disturb the peace of this publick Fair, they shall be taen by order o' the Bailie and Toun Council, and their lugs nailed tae the Tron wi' a twal o' penny nail o' Jock the nailer's making and Rinnan Kerrs nailin' up, and sit down on their bare knees and pray seven times for the King and thrice for the Muckle Laird o' Railton, and pay a groat to me, Matthew Little, Bailie o' the 'foresaid Manor, and now I'll away hame and hae my dinner o' bannock and saut herrin by way o' the auld style;

but must give charge before I gae

*That if auld style should chance to die before another year,
You should chuse out some viliant man, his standard for to bear.'*

Rae Elliot crying the Fair for his first time in 2003

The threat made in the proclamation to nail offenders' "lugs to the Tron wi' a twal o' penny nail" was no idle boast. Jock 'the Nailer' and Rinnan Kerr were two journeymen nailers with George Graham, a respectable nail manufacturer in the town. They would deliver the 'fatal blow' that would drive the twalpenny nail through the land-louper's lug and into the Tron. Apart from this magnified pinprick, the offender would also have to suffer abuse from every honest soul who passed by.

The First Fair, which is cried by the Fair Crier before the Cornet and his supporters leave for the hill, is a rallying call. It summons all who have any claim to the rights and privileges that were awarded by the Court of Session in 1759, to "go out in defence of their property and hear the Proclamation of the Langholm Fair upon the Castle Craigs."

One great border family, the Elliots, has dominated Langholm Common Riding for the last ninety-five years. Christopher 'Kirst' Elliot – a grandnephew of Fair Crier David Hounam – cried the Fair for twenty-three years. He was succeeded by his son, the renowned John 'Popple' Elliot who cried the Fair for thirty-nine years, apart from an enforced break of two years during World War II. 'Popple's' son, John G Elliot was the third generation of Fair Crier, and cried the Fair in Langholm Market Place no fewer than thirty times. The year 2003 saw a fourth generation carry on the family tradition, when Rae Elliot, John's son, cried the Fair for the first time. It was delivered with great authority and passion, to the unbridled delight of all who heard it.

> *'Again I hear the Crier's grim extortions,*
> *And penalty invoked by those who fail,*
> *To keep within conventions sane proportions*
> *Or have their lugs pierced wi' a twal pennynail.'*
>
> Anon

The Riding of the Common, or Marches, became the legal obligation of the Burgesses as decreed by the Court of Session in Edinburgh in 1759.

As already mentioned, Robert, Lord Maxwell, the Earl of Nithsdale bestowed the ten merklands of Langholm upon ten cadets of the Maxwell family in April 1628. These ten men, along with their heirs and tenants, had the right to "win and lead stones off any part of the Common quarries of the said land of Arkinholm", although the Earl himself retained the rights to the woods and fishing.

Common Land was the undivided common property of two or more landowners. In the case of Langholm, the Commonty belonged, in common, to the owners of the ten merklands which bounded it. These owners, along with their heritors and tenants, had certain rights and privileges. These privileges generally included the right to collect anything from it, that might be used as building materials (stones, clay, timber, slates, heather, etc), to harvest it for fuel (usually peat, turf and sometimes wood and coal) and to gather natural vegetation (blossoms, berries and sap crops) to use as food, drinks, and medicines or as fertilisers. This Common Land was also invariably used as common pasture for sheep and cattle in summer, and as a reserve of arable land where an extra crop could be grown. However, no one, whether landowner or tenant, could profit from it; its resources were purely for personal use. For instance, no one could cut timber on it to sell, or rent grazing on it to anyone else. To the lowly peasant, Common land was a God-given natural reserve in times of need; to its owners it could be a great source of frustration, as it represented sometimes vast areas of rough land, which they were powerless to develop or sell.

By 1756, the ownership of the ten merklands of Langholm had changed considerably. Only one Maxwell still had claim to them – John Maxwell of Broomholm who now owned five, but had the common rights to a sixth, previously held by Simon Little of Nittyholm. John Little, a merchant in the town, owned three, and young Henry, third Duke of Buccleuch owned one, but had inherited the sole right to cut timber over the entire Commonty. It would seem that John Maxwell was not content with his lot. The three owners were soon squabbling amongst themselves over where the boundaries of each land lay and what the exact rights were that they all enjoyed.

The Scottish Parliament in 1695 passed an Act called *The Act for the Division of Commonties*, which still remains on the Statute Book today. It allowed a Common to be divided at the instigation of a single pursuer (owner), whether the other parties (joint owners) agreed or not. In this way, much Common Land throughout the country was lost to unscrupulous lairds. In 1500 it was estimated that half the land area of Scotland was Common Land; by the middle of the nineteenth century virtually all of this vast area had become the private property of neighbouring landowners. The Court of Session in Edinburgh was responsible for enforcing this Act and would be arbitrators in any disputes over ownership.

John Maxwell brought an action in the Court of Session against the other owners of the merklands in 1757. He asked that a Commission be set up to examine the lands concerned, and decide for posterity, where the exact boundaries of each land lay. He also asked that the Common be divided up in direct proportion to the value of the lands owned by the various parties. A Commission was formed from eminent men of the area, and they met under oath to consider each claim and counter-claim and the value given to each of the lands concerned. They heard evidence given by five witnesses, local men of advanced years, who each had an intimate knowledge of the lands concerned. Their statements were recorded by a clerk and signed by the witnesses and by each member of the Commission. John Irving was, however, unable to sign his as he could not write. However, a separate Commission had to be set up to consider the issue of the Kilngreen, which Maxwell argued was part of the Common and should therefore be divided. It was pointed out to the Commission that the Kilngreen was smaller than it had been originally. This reduction was brought about by Mr Melville, the Duke's Chamberlain, who had a large wall of stones built at the mouth of the mill dam, in the river Ewes. During the next big flood, the river jumped its banks and afterwards took a new course farther east from the castle walls.

The Court of Session met in Edinburgh in February 1759 to consider the facts and conclusions reached by the local Commissioners who decreed that the Common should be divided up in the proportions of six tenths to John Maxwell, three tenths to John Little and one tenth to the Duke of Buccleuch, but that the latter should retain the right to grow and cut timber over the entire Common.

However, the Division Act stipulated that if a disputed land included mosses, which could not be easily divided, they should remain common, and that access to them should be maintained. The Court therefore decreed that the Common Moss on the north flank of Whita Hill belonged inalienably to the inhabitants of the town, who had the right to cut peats and lead stones from it. The Court also stipulated that a road, twenty feet in breadth, should be maintained to provide unhindered access.

As to the Kilngreen, they decreed that as the townsfolk had used it as free pasture for generations, and as it was the site where the Lamb or Simmer Fair was held, it should remain the property of the town's inhabitants, and that these grazing rights should be maintained.

By far the most important dictate made was that the boundaries of these two areas of Common Land should remain for posterity as they had defined them. That is, the boundaries of the Common should be protected against encroachment from neighbouring landowners. These boundaries were marked by natural objects such as trees or bushes, but where these did not exist, cairns of rough stone were constructed or pits dug. A local man was appointed by the Burgesses to go out each year to inspect these boundaries, and, where necessary, repair the cairns and clean out the pits. He would also report to them any encroachments by neighbouring landowners.

The first man to do this, in about 1765, was Archibald (Bauldy) Beattie, the Town Drummer and Fair Crier and he was credited with carrying out this duty for upwards of fifty years. He would undoubtedly strike a very colourful figure as he strode out toward the hill dressed in his three-cornered hat, drab coat, red plush knee breeches, matching vest and broad-nebbed shoes. His march to the hill, and return from it, would not be accompanied by great bands of music, as it is today; the only sound to set his step by would be the 'tuck' from his own side-drum. Once on the hill, he would point out to all who followed him, the rocks, trees, pits and

cairns, which defined the boundaries of the Common. On reaching the Castle Craigs, the furthermost point on the Common from the town, the party would stop to rest, while Bauldy would take the opportunity to regale them by 'Crying the Fair'. In time a tradition grew up where herrings were roasted on fires kindled at the Castle Craigs on Common Riding day. The herrings were served up with the traditional fare of Barley Bannocks and a "modest quencher of the critter, procured from the native distillery." On his return from the hill, Bauldy would mount the steps beneath the Mercat Cross and 'Cry the Fair' again. This ritual took place on the

quiet day that followed the Simmer or Lamb Fair, and explains how the two unrelated events became linked together.

Bauldy walked the Marches for the last time in 1814, dying in his thatched
cottage at the foot of the Kirk Wynd nine years later at the ripe old age of ninety,
and was buried in the Auld Kirkyard. The Common Riding Committee erected a
tombstone over his grave in 1829. The inscription on it, costing 17/6, pays tribute
to his great dedication in preserving this tradition for posterity.

Peter Graham 'Pete Wheep' succeeded Bauldy Beattie as last Town Drummer
of Langholm.

In 1815, Archie Thomson, an innkeeper in the town, went over the boundaries
on foot and alone. It is the commonly held view that he carried out this duty on
horseback the following year, and therefore must be credited as being the first man
to ride the Common. On that historic day he was accompanied by a small, but
ardent, band of townsmen. However, an article in the *Eskdale and Liddesdale
Advertiser* of August 1886, contradicts this by saying that "in that year (1816)
Messrs John Irving and Frank Beattie rode along with Bauldy Beattie around the
Common. Prior to that date the procession used to go on foot". Whether all three
rode the Common that year or not is open to conjecture.

There have been two instances when the townsfolk of Langholm have risen up 'in
defence o' thir property'. The first occasion, which became known as 'The Kilngreen
Incident', happened on Friday 15th December 1816. It was precipitated by Mr
Archibald Scott, Writer, who attempted to extend his garden at Clinthead onto the
Kilngreen by planting a number of small trees and by cutting a trench beyond them as
the foundation for a wall. The townsfolk saw this as a flagrant encroachment onto
land that was theirs 'by right and lot', so an angry mob stormed the garden and pulled
up some of the young trees. On the following day a procession, armed with spades
and long poles and led by Peter Graham, Town Drummer, returned to the enclosure
and proceeded to pull up the remaining young trees. These trees were then tied to the
long poles and carried triumphantly through the streets. The ringleaders of the mob,
William Beattie, George Graham, Archie Thomson and David Hounam were arrested
and charged with Mobbing and Rioting. They all appeared before Sir Thomas
Kirkpatrick in Dumfries Sheriff Court, where the prosecution claimed that the ground
in question was the property of the Duke of Buccleuch and that he had given the
owner permission to close it in four years before this. The defence claimed that: -

> 'the Kilngreen is an ancient place where clay is got,
> and it belongs to us by right and lot'

and that the people of Langholm had been in the habit of riding the Marches of the
different Commonties once a year from time immemorial. This is a startling statement
to make under oath in a Court of Law for, if it is true, it completely contradicts the
notion that the Marches were ridden for the first time in 1816, implying that riding
the Marches was, in 1816, a time honoured tradition!

The case dragged on for three days, and in the end the Sheriff found the
defendants liable for the damage done and the expenses of the action. The four
men were ordered to pay twenty pounds each, which they all did except for David
Hounam who bluntly refused to pay one penny. Scott threatened to put him in jail
if he did not pay his dues, but Davie sent a message back saying "Tell Mr Scott frae
mie that aw wadna pay him a penny if his tongue wiz hingin' oot!" Therefore,

Davie was sent on an enforced vacation to Dumfries Jail. However, he soon won the respect of the Governor who, on discovering that he was a weaver to trade, had a hand loom and web brought into the prison. Davie set happily to work weaving, with the help of an army deserter who wound his bobbins. Mr Scott soon relented, and Davie was released from prison. The Kilngreen incident, and how Davie avoided paying his dues, became a standing joke in the town. David Hounam replaced 'Pete Wheep' as Fair Crier in 1858, and died in 1877 at the age of eighty-seven, after leading a colourful and eventful life.

Messrs William Beattie, Robert Brown, John Irving and Archibald Thomson, who were known collectively as 'The Fathers of the Common Riding', first introduced horse racing into the Common Riding in 1816. The year 1834 saw a break with this tradition, for it was in this year that the horse racing and sports were moved from the Kilngreen and onto the Castleholm, or 'Big Kilngreen' as it was sometimes known. Horse racing formed only a small part of the Common Riding programme in those days, for as well as foot running, wrestling and high jumping there were also other popular old-fashioned country sports such as 'climbing the greasy pole' and 'chasing the well-soaped pig'.

Ex-Cornet Jimmy Paterson arriving at the Monument during the Foot and Mouth Common Riding of 1952

Another milestone was reached in 1817 when the first Master of Ceremonies or Cornet was selected. The first man to receive this honour was W Pasley, a manufacturer in the town. He was followed on the day by about half a dozen mounted supporters, as well as others on foot, but the identity of this first Cornet has always been shrouded in mystery. The *Census Records of 1841* for the Parish of Langholm show the most likely candidate to be one William Pasley, a Cotton Manufacturer in the Town, who resided at 23 Kirk Wynd. He would have been in his mid-fifties when he carried out this duty, and would probably be picked because of the standing he had in the town as a respected local businessman.

Up until 1871 the name Cornet referred to the lowest rank of commissioned officer in a British Cavalry Regiment, his duty being to guard and parade the ensign or regimental colours. When Ian Earsman carried out this duty in 2003, he was the 174th Cornet to have led his mounted supporters round the ancient Commonty. However, it should be noted that six Cornets have, for various reasons, carried out this duty more than once, the most notable being Cornet Jimmy Paterson of Terrona who carried the flag no fewer than eight times.

In 1837 Cornet Jimmy Clark, a saddler, set another precedent by being the first to lead his followers round the newly-finished Monument which crowned Whita Hill.

Originally only men residing in the Old Town of Langholm were eligible to carry out this duty, as only they had any claim to the rights and privileges that were awarded by the Court of Session in 1759. The third Duke of Buccleuch had given the residents of New Langholm their own grazing and fuel rights on certain areas of land, but the ownership of this land was never disputed. This tradition was broken for the first time in 1843 when a blacksmith, Robert Anderson, became the first Meikleholmer (a resident of the New Town) chosen to be Cornet.

In 1890 a public meeting to elect a Cornet by a simple show of hands was held for the first time and this system continued until 1920 when the first public ballot was introduced.

There have been quite a number of instances of Cornets coming from two or even three generations of the same family. The most notable example of this was the Irving family. When David Irving of Langholm Mill was elected Cornet in Queen Victoria's Diamond Jubilee year of 1897, his elder brother, father, cousin and two uncles had already preceded him. His grandfather, John Irving of Langholm Mill, had been one of the 'Fathers of the Common Riding', that small band of local men who first rode the Marches in 1816. However, this great run did not end with his appointment; for eight years later his younger brother, Simon filled the office. The Irvings are unique in the annals of Common Riding lore in that they can claim to have supplied the town with seven Cornets from two successive generations of one family! David Irving also had the distinction of being the last Cornet to receive the flag from in front of the Crown Hotel, then the headquarters of the Common Riding. He was also the last to carry the old style of flag, the one replacing it being the first to have the burgh coat of arms incorporated into its design. In 1967, he celebrated his Seventieth Jubilee, and to mark the occasion received a medallion from the Langholm Ex-Cornets Association and an inscribed clock from the Common Riding Committee. At the Concert and Investiture, the ninety-one-year old confessed to the audience that he "didn't know much about making speeches", but asked that they join him in singing *Keep Right on to the*

End of the Road. They did, and when the song finished there was scarcely a dry eye left in the hall.

Ex-Cornet David Irving (front) celebrating his Seventieth Jubilee in 1967

To be Cornet is one of the greatest honours Langholm can bestow on its sons, and a steady stream of young men still put their names forward in the hope they will be picked to fill the office. The Cornet is a heroic symbol of both the past and the present, and the epitome of a thousand boyhood dreams. However, this great honour carries with it heavy responsibility, for on the day he represents a tradition which is looked upon by many with a reverence akin to religion.

The Flag or Burgh Standard is the emblem of the Cornet's office. It is jealously guarded and very rarely seen in public, other than on Common Riding Day. After receiving it from the Officiating Magistrate (Provost) on Common Riding morning, the Cornet parades it around the town before his spectacular gallop up the Kirk Wynd and on to the hill. There are few sights more pleasing to a local's eye than to see the sun dance over its golden surface as it flutters in the warm summer breeze. Once at the Castle Craigs, the flag may be handed to the Semi-Jubilee Cornet to carry round the Monument and down to Whita Well. But from then on, it is the sole property of the Cornet, and like some ancient religious artefact, it is treated with a respect which borders almost on veneration.

The procession to mark the return of the flag to the Town Hall at dusk is a truly awe-inspiring and moving spectacle. At no other time is the pride and love for this 'wee bit toon' more overwhelming. As the swifts pirouette overhead, the emblems dance and the massive throng sings the "auld, auld sang", the Burgh Standard is reluctantly handed back until the next time this glorious day dawns.

The people of Langholm owe a great debt of gratitude to the Scott family who, from 1898, have generously donated each successive Burgh Flag to the town. In 1898, Alex Scott of Erkinholme presented the first, a hand-painted silk flag, which was carried by Cornet John W Church, the first Cornet to receive the flag from outside the Town Hall. Cornet John Wallace carried the second flag, presented by James A Scott of Erkinholme in 1907, while the third was presented in 1935 by Arthur M Scott of Eskmount, and carried by Cornet C Stewart Paisley. In 1950, Cornet John M Young carried the new flag which was presented by William Sutton Scott of The Glen. Thirty-eight years later, in 1988, Cornet Andrew J Jeffrey was the first to carry the current flag gifted to the town by Dr Tom Scott.

To say that only Cornets have carried the Flag round the Common is not strictly true, for there is an exception to every rule. At the Common Riding in 1916, the 'City Fathers' refused to allow the Flag to be used, as they felt the Common Riding should be curtailed as a mark of respect to those local lads fighting abroad. It should be remembered that only three weeks had passed since the start of the Battle of the Somme, when 60,000 British troops were either killed, wounded or went missing on the first day of fighting. Some Common Riding worthies managed to get an old and frail Flag, and it was this Cornet John Wilson carried up the Kirk Wynd. However, on reaching the top he decided to go no further, and it was rolled up and handed to a young boy, Robert McCracken, to carry on foot round the hill. He was thirteen years old at the time, and so was the youngest person ever to carry the Flag round the Common.

The Common Ridings of the Border towns have aspects which make each of them unique; one of the most notable features at the Langholm Common Riding is the carrying of emblems in the procession.

Of the four, the one with the most obvious use is the Spade, which leads the procession on Common Riding Day. Bedecked with heather and 'anointed wi' whisky' at a select ceremony before the Common Riding, it is carried by the Spade Carrier, who uses it to cut sods at various points to mark the boundaries of the Common Land.

In 1866 no fewer than sixteen sods were cut, while Hyslop in *Langholm as It Was* (first published in 1912) lists only eight. He quite rightly stressed the need to write down for posterity where each site was. One site was at Bet's Thorn, which grew in Walter Ballantyne's garden, between the Buccleuch Hotel and Ashley Bank Lodge. If these sods marked the boundaries of the two remaining areas of Common Land left after the division of the Commonty in 1759, it is difficult to see how this Thorn could mark the boundary of either the Kilngreen or Common Moss. Perhaps it predated this and was one of the natural objects, which defined the limits of the original Langholm Common. The fact that two sods were, and still are, cut on the Castleholm may cause confusion.

But it should be remembered that the Duke's Chamberlain changed the course of the River Ewes, making it flow further east from the Castle. This meant that land that was once part of the Kilngreen now lay on the other side of the river, on the Castleholm.

Today sods are cut at the following points on the Marches: -

1. Below the first cairn, after entering the Common Moss through the boundary gate.
2. At the south side of the Monument on top of Whita Hill.
3. At the south end of the Kilngreen, behind the Townhead Tollbar.
4. At the north end of the Castleholm, near to Ewes Bridge.
5. At the south end of Castleholm near to 'the meeting of the waters'.

Harry Erskine,
Spade Carrier from
1966 to 1982

The question will have been asked, no doubt, why does the spade not make an appearance at the 'Handing-in Ceremony' at night? One explanation put forward is that it was simply not available, as it was auctioned off to the highest bidder in the yard of the Crown Hotel at lunchtime on Common Riding day. From the money raised, the Spade Carrier was expected to buy a new spade for the next year.

Next in the procession comes the Barley Bannock and Saut Herring, the most obscure of all the emblems but the one that seems to typify Langholm the most. It has been suggested that the Barley Banna' is a symbol of the people's feudal dues to the local Baron, and therefore relates more to the Fair than the Common Riding itself. Every farmer or cultivator of the soil was bound by the objectionable feudal law of 'thirlage' to get their oats or bere (barley) ground at a particular baronial mill, and to pay the Baron (and miller!) a 'multure', or duty for the privilege of doing so. The Thirlage Act of 1799 commuted this to an undertaking to make an annual payment, which was known as a 'dry multure'. In the case of Langholm, this dry multure was a Bannock, which was collected by the Bailie on Simmer Fair Day. The Baronial Mill of Langholm was Langholm Mill, at the foot of the Chapel Path.

Hyslop in *Langholm As It Was* has suggested that the Saut Herrin' represents the Baron's right to the fisheries, just as the Bannock represents his right to the mills, or it could simply be relish to spice up the otherwise dry bannock.

Barley Bannocks and Herrings also played a part in ancient Scottish Hallowe'en ritual. If a person retired to bed, without drinking, after eating a heavily salted Barley Bannock (or one laced with soot!), or a whole, stolen herring, their future spouse would appear to them in a prophetic dream! The eating of Barley Bannocks and drinking of whisky also played an important part in the ancient Celtic Festival of Beltane.

The nail used to crucify the fish to the platter is the 'twalpenny nail' mentioned in the Fair, and used to nail offenders' lugs to the Tron in the Market Place. The term twalpenny nail (twelve-penny nail) refers to the system for grading nail sizes. By this convention, a twelve-penny nail was originally $3^1/4$ inches long. The word 'twelve-penny' is derived from the cost in pennies of buying one hundred such nails.

John Jeffrey, local blacksmith and engineer, making a Twalpenny nail in 1986

The most spectacular emblem is the giant Scots Thistle – MacDiarmid's "Mony brainchin' candelabra", which "dances doon the street like a livin' trie". Being the national emblem of Scotland it is both defensive and aggressive, and may have been adopted as a warning to those who dared 'wound' the town. For many years the thistle was grown in a garden at the Townfoot. However, today the growing of the thistle is open to competition. The Thistle Bearer selects the best specimen from those available, while the Cornet and Committee ratify this choice when they inspect the emblem on Simmer Fair Night.

To carry the Thistle requires great strength and endurance.

Yiddie Bally (Ballantyne), a character in a short story by Hugh MacDiarmid, was a Thistle Bearer who, unfortunately, possessed neither of these qualities:

For Yiddie was a puir eaten-an'-spewed up lookin' critur a' his days. But even afore hie left the schule hie was Common-Riding daft, leeved for naething else, and threw himsel wholehertedly intae it. As a committee member ee couldna' hae wish'd for better; hie was hard workin', conscientious and totally selfless. When it came tae Common Riding statistics, folklore and protocol hie was unrivalled; he was like the memory man in the peepur, only the Common Riding was Yiddie's 'specialist subject'. But deep doon hie harboured a dream – a special, but impossible dream – tae cairry the Thistle. Then yin year fate smiled on him, for Neen Ferguson, the principal cairrier, took tae his bed wi flu and a volunteer was sought tae cairry the Thistle frae the fit o' the Port intae the Mairket Place – a distance o' aboot a hunner yairds. Yiddie announced that "Hie wad cairry the thistle!" Well they tried lang and hard tae discourage him by sayin' that frae the general standpoint o' the programme the Thistle should be weel and truly cairret. But it was nae use, for hie had them in a very awkward position as his word was almost law, and there was nae way hie was gaen tae back doon. "I'm no' muckle tae look at but I've niver let the Common Riding doon yit throuw onything I've dune or left undune – an' I'll no' let the Thistle doon neither. I'll ha'e ma helpers, but frae the fit o' the Port tae the middle o' the Mairket Place I'll cairry it myself, an' nae ither man'll pit a fingur on the pole!"

Well, excitement was runnin' high when the big day dawned and Yiddie was tae the fore at the cuttin', wi the holder for the pole strappit roon his waist. It was a massive brute, and when Yiddie took the strain his puir frame fair doubled under the load, were it no for his helpers lending their support his spine wad hae cracked wi' every step. But his nemesis was fast approaching – for they were soon at the fit o' the Port. "Noo, haunds aff! I'll manage the rest misel". It was wonderfu' tae see hoo the wie critur braced himsel, Heaven only kens what hie maun hae been sufferin'. Hie steckered forit as the massive weed tottered abune him. It was a case o' the pride o' the Common Riding verus his ain, could hie maintain them baith? There was only yin way oot – he sterted tae rin! Mercifully hie reached his goal, the middle o' the Mairket Place, afore he crumpled and fell beneath the mirad o' jags. Then all hell was let loose. "Gangway" somebody shouted, as a lane opened up tae the door o' the Chemist's shop. Yin man cairret him tae the doorstep o' the shop while everybody else stood roon like stookies. "Gang on wi' the Common Riding" he cried in a voice that soondit right roon the Mairket Place. And they did. But Yiddie died afore his voice stoppit echoing – an' whiles I think it hasna stoppit yit.

The 'Bonnie Rose Croon' was the last emblem to be added to the proceedings, probably sometime in the early nineteenth century. The Crown is thought to be a symbol of kinship and loyalty, two qualities that exist in abundance at Langholm Common Riding, and signifies the way Langholm crowns itself each Common Riding day. It has been suggested that the Crown may also symbolise the strong connections the Common Riding has with the Crown Hotel. This tie is further highlighted by the existence of a crown on several of the old flags.

The Crown is painstakingly made each year from thousands of Sweet William or Rambler Rose blossoms individually tied onto a metal frame, which is wrapped in wet sphagnum moss to prevent the flowers from drying out. The whole structure is topped by a 'toorie' of orange lilies and white heather, which is pushed onto a metal spike protruding from its top. It takes four people two and a half days to make the Crown and after many hours of dedicated work, its appearance on the day is eagerly awaited.

Three members of the Murray family have made the Crown no less than forty times in the last forty-one years. The late Ex-Cornet Ian Murray first made the Crown in 1963, and in 1978 his sister, the late Mrs Ella Patterson took over the job. Ian's son, Leslie, who made his first crown in 1985, in turn succeeded her. The only break with this tradition was in 1975 when Mrs Irene Bell made it.

Leslie Murray making the Crown

One of the best-loved traditions of Langholm Common Riding is the carrying of Heather Besoms by the children in the procession. In her book, *From Dawn to Dusk*, Mrs Betty Little states that this custom originated in 1894 when Mr Robert McGeorge offered a prize to the boy who returned from the hill with the best bunch of heather. It seems that this competition was not particularly well received by the boys, until the incentive of a threepenny piece for each competitor was added the following year. Due to spiralling inflation over the last 110 years, this payment has

Sybil Hardie and John Young with their heather besoms
one "slootery" Common Riding in the early 1930s

now been increased to a shiny twenty pence piece! However, the starting date of 1894 is contradicted in a paper submitted to the Hawick Archaeological Society by its President, Mr Robert Murray in 1866. In it he eloquently describes his visit to Langholm Common Riding that year and mentions seeing in the procession "fifty cheerful boys waving little heather brooms, which their willing hands had made". Clearly, the heather besom parade is much older than was originally thought. The element of competition has been recently re-introduced, when the Langholm and District Scotch Pie Club (a group of local pie enthusiasts) offered a prize for the best traditional heather besom.

Another custom unique to Langholm Common Riding is the manner by which the Common Riding Colours are picked each year. The colours of the official ties and rosettes and the ribbons that decorate the brow bands and martingales of the Cornet's horse and the emblems are the racing colours of the owner of the winning horse of that year's Epsom Derby. How this came about is open to debate and a number of different theories have found favour over the years. The practice was in vogue in the 1880s and there is some evidence that it may have been started in the early part of that decade. One of the most widely held views is that it was adopted in 1883 when St Blaise, a horse belonging to Sir Frederick Johnstone of Westerhall and his racing partner Lord Alington, won the Derby. A second horse from this stable, Common won the race in 1891 under the same trainer, John Porter. Common went on to achieve 'the triple' by also winning The St Leger and 2,000 Guineas that year.

It has been suggested that the Derby colours may have been unofficially adopted in 1883, but that the practice was not officially recognised by the Common Riding Committee until 1907. Several attempts have been made to standardise the colours, but these have met with little support from the people of the town. No doubt the outcome of this great Epsom Classic will be looked forward to by Langholm folk for many years to come.

It is not possible to over-emphasise the part music plays in Langholm Common Riding, for the town's three local Bands collectively lift the whole proceedings to a higher plane. From the moment the silence is broken by the shrill strains of flutes echoing around the empty streets, until that tearful moment fully fourteen hours later when the Town Band plays the 'auld, auld sang' one last time, the Common Riding and the Bands are as one. For nothing can gladden the heart of the Langholmite, the way the beloved Common Riding airs can. When played or sung at times of great exhilaration, or indeed sadness, they reach into the deepest recesses of the soul and re-ignite the flame of passion that burns inside for this 'Spot Supremely Blest' and its hallowed traditions.

The Flute Band is the harbinger of the Common Riding, and is unique in that it only performs in public twice a year! The players muster for the first time on Simmer Fair Night when they gather at the Townfoot to meet exiles returning home for the Common Riding on the last train back into the town. That the 9.15 pm train stopped running into Langholm in the mid-1950s is of little, or no, concern to them for the Common Riding is predominantly about the past. Eight short hours later, at 5 o' clock in the morning, they muster again at the Townfoot before perambulating the town to waken the residents from their slumbers. Then it is off to the Hound Trail on the side of Whita Hill, via the Lamb Hill, with a short stop for a welcome glass of rum and milk at Hillhead Cottage.

Like so many things pertaining to the Common Riding, the origins of the Flute Band are shrouded in mystery. Although it first played at the Common Riding in 1862, it is thought to be a great deal older than this. Betty Little points out in *From Dawn to Dusk* that as Langholm had a Town Drummer before 1759 it would not be unreasonable to assume that the complement to this, a fife or flute player, would also have existed, and from this would have grown a flute and drum band.

The Flute Band in 1925

No records exist of when the Flute Band first met 'The Last Train.' However, this tradition was described as being "long-established" in reports from the 1890s. In 1913, the Pipe Band attended the station as well. While two years later in 1915, there were drums, triangles but only two flutes in attendance, and it was suggested by the local press, "It would be better to dispense with the music."

Today, the Flute Band is the largest band in the town. On the Simmer Fair Night in 2003, the total complement in the band included twenty-six flautists, twenty-five triangle players, two side drummers and a base drummer. Three triangles were also kept for the Cornets to play 'up the street' from the 'Toonfit' to the Buck Hotel, and back again to the Town Hall.

The Pipe Band adds a stirring and patriotic flavour to the proceedings. It also fulfils another important function by leading the heather besom parade. The earliest recollection many will have is of carrying their heather besom up the street behind the Pipe Band, so this band plays a major part in stimulating the fertile mind of the bairn who will grow into the ardent Langholmite of tomorrow. They in turn will carry or push their own children up the street – and so the cycle continues as the tradition is handed on down through the generations.

The Pipe Band is the youngest of the three bands. An article in the *Eskdale and Liddesdale Advertiser* of March 1972 entitled "Langholm query – What is the oldest Pipe Band in the Borders?" suggests that the Pipe Band was formed in 1900 when four local volunteers, who had been serving in Africa during the early stages of the Boer War, returned to Langholm on leave. At that time there were several individuals in the town who were pipers, one of whom was the late Provost John Ewart, and it was he who suggested to his fellow pipers that they meet the train at Langholm Station to play the four volunteers up the High Street.

The bagpipes have a very long pedigree, dating from the prehistoric shawms and hornpipes of near Eastern civilisations. Pipes were being played in the Highlands of

Scotland by 1400, and the most recognisable form, the Scottish or Highland pipes, had replaced the harp as the traditional musical instrument of Gaelic Society by the late sixteenth century. The piper held a much-esteemed position in the Highland Clan system and played in their Great Halls to praise Chieftains and warriors, and to lament their passing. One great dynasty of clan pipers, the MacCrimmons, were credited with bringing about a renaissance in pipe music by raising it to the classical and complicated structure known in Gaelic as Piobaireachd (meaning piping, but pronounced Pibroch). In the Lowlands, the Scottish Smallpipes along with the harp were the chief musical instruments of reiving times and, when not being played on their own, were used to accompany the singing of traditional Border Ballads.

In battle the war pipes were without equal as weapons of terror and were said to be worth one hundred guns. Their shrill and penetrating notes rose over the roar and din of battle and it has been claimed that pipes have been heard over a distance of six miles – or even ten miles under favourable conditions. During the Great War, over a thousand pipers died in that terrible conflict. Armed only with their pipes, they led their comrades 'over the top' and into murderous fire, and their bravery earned them the nickname "The Ladies from Hell" from the enemy. One Border piper, Daniel Laidlaw of 7th Battalion of the King's Own Scottish Borderers was awarded the VC for his great bravery during the Battle of Loos in September 1915. Seeing that his companions were severely shaken by a heavy bombardment of artillery and gas shells, he pulled off his gas mask and, with complete disregard for his safety, mounted the parapet of the trench and rallied his men to the strains of *Blue Bonnets o'er the Border* and the Regimental Charge, *Standards on the Braes o' Mar*. Unarmed and under hellish enemy machine-gun fire, he led the advance on the German frontline on Hill 70, but was wounded and fell before reaching it. He continued to play his men forward until that position was won.

The sound of the pipes, it was once claimed, "is a call to battle, a lament or the awakening of memories that recall a time lost and a land that will call to the heart of anyone with Scottish Blood!"

It has been claimed that Langholm Town Band is the oldest brass band in Scotland, if not in Britain. However, this bold statement needs further elaboration. Although the St Ronan's Silver Band from Innerleithen can claim to be older, being founded as a fyfe and drum band in 1810, its successor, the Innerleithen and Traquair Brass Band fell away for a number of years before being resurrected. It is probably more correct to say that of all the brass bands in Scotland, the Langholm Town Band has been in existence for the longest *continuous* period of time. When the remnants of the Scots Greys passed triumphantly through Langholm in July 1817, they were played through the streets by "a band of music lately formed in the town". Legend has it that the Commanding Officer was so impressed with the band's performance that he presented them with part of the buckle from his horse's harness. However, Beattie in *Lang Syne in Eskdale* claims that this badge pre-dated the Scots Greys visit and was first worn by the band's drummer in 1815. This same man wore it when the band welcomed the Scots Greys home, two years later. In 1898 the badge's owner, Mrs Irving of the Laird's Entry, gave the badge to Bandmaster Balfour, and he wore it in his hat at the Common Riding that year. Illustrated on the next page is the object known as the 'Band Buckle', which now has pride of place among other relics in Langholm Town Hall.

In March 1816, the local Lodge of Freemasons, Lodge Eskdale Kilwinning, made the gift of five guineas to a "band of musicians, lately established here" to allow them to engage a teacher and to purchase instruments, the proviso being that they would play for them, free gratis, at their procession on St John's Day, or at any other time. However, a year earlier in August 1815, the Langholm Band of Music played Lord Lynedock, the hero of Barossa and Aide-de-Camp to Sir John Moore at Corunna, triumphantly through the streets of the town, playing some favourite and patriotic airs.

Clearly the band was in existence before this; one source quotes 1813 as the year of its inception, although this is open to debate.

It should be pointed out that the early band would contain no brass instruments, as brass instruments only appeared in civil bands in Britain around the middle of the nineteenth century. It was in the late 1840s that the Belgian, Adolphe Sax, patented a family of valved brass instruments (including the saxophone and saxhorn), which were the precursors of modern brass instruments. In the 1860s, when William A Anderson wielded the baton as conductor, the band consisted of a mixture of woodwind and brass, bands composed entirely of brass instruments appearing at a later date.

The Town Band plays a pivotal role in the Common Riding day's proceedings. After the Cornet receives the Town's Standard from the Officiating Magistrate, the Band leads him and his followers through the streets to the strains of *O' A' the Airts*, a Burns' song that replaced *Scots Wha Hae* sometime after 1886.

Immediately after the First Fair is cried, the Band leads the people up the Kirk Wynd to the strains of the *Rose of Allandale*. After the horsemen's spectacular gallop on to the hill, the Band again plays this air from the old EU Kirk to the Market Place, before making its way to the Townfoot to escort the two remaining emblems, the Thistle and the Crown, back to Mount Hooley. The lyrics to *Allandale* were written by Charles Jeffreys and first appeared in print in 1835.

Although it has been claimed that *The Rose of Allandale* was the name of a ship, the song probably refers to the voyage that a young couple undertook through life. The Allandale in question was a village to the west of Bonnybridge in Stirlingshire and not a community near Hexham, Northumberland, as is sometimes thought.

The Flo'ers o' the Forest, the air played by the Band on the return from the Townfoot with the emblems, was first played in 1878 in the garden of Wullie Ir'in (Irving) 'honest man', prior to the Thistle being cut. Wullie grew this emblem for many years, and also made the Crown, but died six weeks before the Common Riding that year.

On their triumphant return, the Band leads the Cornet and his mounted followers down the Kirk Wynd, along the High Street, and back to the crowded Market Place to hear the Second Fair cried. On this occasion, the tune played is *Thou Bonnie Woods o' Craigielea*. Like most airs played at Langholm Common Riding, *Craigielea* has no real connection with the town, and was probably adopted by the band when a popular 'hit' of the day. The "Craigielea" of the title is an area to the northwest of Paisley, and it is worth noting that *Craigielea* is reputed to have been the tune on which *Waltzing Matilda* is based, after being 'misremembered' by its composer, Christina McPherson.

After the Second Fair has been cried, the multitude, both on horseback and on foot, join hands as *Auld Lang Syne* is sung with great poignancy, and this is the air the Band plays as it leads the procession back up the Kirk Wynd and on to Drove Road. The procession again comes to a brief halt at the bottom of Alma Place when the Band members regale everyone by **singing** the first verse of *Jeannie's Black E'e* – the narrowness of the road making instrument playing impossible!

Langholm Town Band at Mount Hooley during the Common Riding of 1889
On the extreme right is the bandmaster, William "auld Ca'vert"

The appearance of the emblems, the Cornet and his mounted supporters on the Bar Brae, to the accompaniment of *Annie Laurie* and *On the Banks of Allan Water*, is another highlight of the day.

At night, the Band marches to the dance on the green to the strains of *Jeannie's Black E'e* and *Scotland Yet* – the only song to have any real local connection. As the sun begins to set behind Meikleholm, the Cornet and his Right and Left Hand Men mount up behind the Band and, with the multitude and emblems, begin to wend their way slowly homeward to the strains of *Auld Lang Syne*. It is at this point that many thoughts are cast back to Common Ridings of yore, and to kith and kin that have gone. The procession halts at the Kilngreen where old and young form rings and dance the Common Riding Polka, to the tune *The Merry Elves*. Once completed the procession reforms and makes its way to the Crown Hotel where a second Polka is danced, with even greater abandon. A third Polka is danced at the Townfoot, near the site of the old Buccleuch Hotel, and when the Cornet, Band and emblems re-enter the Market Place through 'the Straits' it seems as if half the world has packed itself into that ancient Square. The Flag is returned 'unstained and unsullied', as heart-felt words are spoken and tears well up in many eyes. Hands are warmly clasped again as the 'auld, auld sang' is sung one last time, and another memorable Common Riding slips from grasp and into the past.

The Common Riding cannot be described adequately in words, for as an old saying goes "It's better felt than telt".

It is the day when Langholm as it was, and Langholm as it is, meet for a few brief moments before taking their separate roads again. The Common Riding is a passion born out of civic pride and love and out of a longing for days and folk that are gone. In its traditions Langholm folk glory in their rich and bloody past, while in their young Cornet they look forward with glowing optimism to the future.

The future of this Common Riding is assured, for its foundations are built on the bedrock of time-honoured tradition. At its end, as the dying strains of *Auld Lang Syne* drift out to the hills and into the past, the author, for one, is 'mighty proud' to have been born in a town which guards its ancient customs … "with a miser's care".

> *'Tis the shrine where our hearts keep returning*
> *Wherever our feet may be led;*
> *All our love on that altar lies burning,*
> *All our song-wreaths around it are spread.'*

The Land We Love
by Will H Ogilvie

Bibliography

ALEXANDER, David M. *The Wallace Family and Langholm*, David Alexander 1999.

ALMACK, Edward A. *The History of the Second Dragoons "Royal Scots Greys"*, London 1908.

ANON. *County of Dumfries, Census Records of 1841 by surname, Parish of Langholm (Parts 1 & 2)*, Dumfries and Galloway Family History Society 2002.

ARMSTRONG, John A. *The Story of Langholm Castle*, The Armstrong Clan Trust.

ARMSTRONG, Robert Bruce *The History of Liddesdale, Eskdale, Ewesdale, Wauchopedale and the Debatable Lands (Part 1)*, David Douglas, Edinburgh 1883.

ARMSTRONG, William A. *The Armstrong Borderland*, John McQueen & Son Ltd, Galashiels 1960.

BARNARD, Alfred *The Whisky Distilleries of the United Kingdom*, London 1887.

BEATTIE, David J. *Lang Syne in Eskdale*, Charles Thurnam & Sons Ltd, Carlisle 1950.

BEATTIE, David J. *Prince Charlie and the Borderland*, Charles Thurnam & Sons, Carlisle 1928.

BEATTIE, David J. *Oor Ain Folk*, Charles Thurnam & Sons Ltd, Carlisle 1933.

BEATTIE, David J. *It Happened Then – Stray Notes of Lang Syne*, Langholm Reference Library.

BEATTIE, James *Westerkirk Parish &surrounding areas - historical notes*, (transcribed or original articles collected or written by) County Library, Langholm.

BELL, Walter *Langholm RFC 1871-1971 – Langholm's First Hundred*, LRFC 1972.

BETTS, Colin *Eskdalemuir - The Book*, Floating World, Pengrain, Eskdalemuir 1998.

BOLD, Alan *MacDiarmid*, John Murray (Publishers) Ltd, 50 Albemarle Street, London 1988.

BOGG, Edmund — *A Thousand Miles of Wandering in the Border Country,* Publishers: Mawson, Swan & Morgan, Newcastle and John Sampson, York 1898.

BURTON, Anthony — *Thomas Telford,* Aurum Press Ltd, London 1999.

BYERS, John — *Liddesdale - Historical and Descriptive,* John McQueen & Son Ltd, Galashiels, 1952.

COLE, J.R. — *A Survey of the Debatable Land and Glen Tarras 1449-1620,* Thesis submitted to the University of Manchester for Degree of Master of Arts, 1982.

DONNACHIE, Ian — *Industrial Archaeology of Galloway (South-west Scotland including Wigtown, Kirkcudbright and parts of Dumfries),* David & Charles, Newton Abbot, Devon 1971.

EDDINGTON, Alexander — *Castles and Historic Homes of the Border,* Oliver & Boyd, Edinburgh and London 1949.

ELLIOT, Walter et al — *The Borders Book,* Birlinn Ltd, Edinburgh 1995.

FRASER, George MacDonald — *The Steel Bonnets,* Barrie & Jenkins, London 1971.

GRIFFITHS, John — *The Phoenix Book of International Rugby Records,* J. M. Dent & Sons Ltd, London and Melbourne 1987.

HYSLOP, John & Robert — *Langholm As It Was,* Hills & Co, Sunderland 1912.

LANG, Jean — *A Land of Romance,* Thomas Nelson & Sons Ltd, Edinburgh & London 1910.

LAW, Graham et al — *Tennent's Velvet Rugby Record - 1998/99,* SRU Publications Department, Murrayfield, Edinburgh.

LITTLE, Betty — *From Dawn to Dusk – The Story of Langholm Common Riding,* Eskdale and Liddesdale Newpapers Ltd, Langholm 1997.

MACLAREN, Muir — *Meat & Music – Stories from the Valley of the Liddel,* The Jedburgh Press 1988.

MARTIN, Rev. Thomas et al — *The Statistical Account of Scotland 1791-99, Vol. 4 (Dumfriesshire),* E.P. Publishing Ltd, East Ardsley, Wakefield, UK, 1978 (re-issued).

MARSDEN, John — *The Illustrated Border Ballads,* MacMillan Ltd, London 1990.

MASSIE, Allan — *101 Great Scots,* W & R Chambers Ltd, Edinburgh 1987.

MAXWELL-IRVING, Alastair M.T. — *The Border Towers of Scotland, Their History and Architecture – The West March,* Maxwell-Irving, Dumfries 2000.

McCARTNEY, R Bruce — *The Railway to Langholm – An illustrated record,* Cairndhu Publications, Langholm 1991.

MICKLE, William Julius — *Poems and a Tragedy,* printed by A. Paris, Roll's Buildings, for E. Edgerton, Charing Cross; William Richardson, Royal Exchange & Flecher & Hanwell, Oxford 1794.

MOFFAT, Alistair — *The Borders – A History of the Borders from Earliest Times,* Deerpark Press, Selkirk 2002.

MORRISON, Brenda et al — *The Ewes Valley*, Cairndhu Publications, Langholm 2000.

MURRAY, Robert — *Hawick Songs and Song Writers, (Second Edition)*, W & J Kennedy, Hawick 1889.

OGILVIE, Will H. — *The Land We Love (Third Edition)*, Fraser, Asher & Co, Ltd, Glasgow & Dalbeattie.

OLIVER, Thomas — *A Visit to Langholm & the History of its Manufactures*, John McQueen & Son Ltd, Galashiels 1942.

PASLEY, Rodney — *'Send Malcolm!' The Life of Major-General Sir John Malcolm 1769-1833*, The British Association for Cemeteries in South Asia 1982.

RIDDELL, Henry Scott — *The Poetical Works of Henry Scott Riddell (Volume 1)*, Maurice Ogle & Co, Glasgow 1871.

RUSSELL, James A — *The Book of Dumfriesshire*, Blacklock Farries & Sons Ltd, Dumfries 1964.

SCOTT, Sir Walter — *The Minstrelsy of the Scottish Border*, Ward Lock & Co London.

SPEIRS, Laing — *The Border League Story*, Scottish Borders Rugby Union, Galashiels 2000.

THOMSON, J. H — *The Martyr Graves of Scotland*, Oliphant, Anderson & Ferrier, Edinburgh & London.

TOWNSEND, Brian — *Scotch Missed – The Lost Distilleries of Scotland*, Neil Wilson Publishing Ltd, Glasgow 1993.

TRANTER, Nigel — *Portrait of the Border Country*, Robert Hale & Co, London 1972.

VARIOUS — *Eastern Dumfriesshire – an Archaeological Landscape*, RCAHMS, The Stationery Office, Edinburgh 1997.

WATSON, Godfrey — *The Border Reivers*, Robert Hale & Co 1974.

WATT, R. H. — *Langholm Old Parish Church*, The Times Printing Works, Motherwell 1946

WELSH, Matthew — *Maggie Elliot, A Romance of the Ewes and other Poems*, Robert Scott, Langholm, John Menzies & Co, Ltd, Edinburgh & Glasgow.

WILKINS, Frances — *Dumfries and Galloway's Smuggling Story*, Wyre Forest Press 1993.

WILSON, John Mackay — *Tales of the Borders (and of Scotland)*, William P. Nimmo, Edinburgh.

WILSON, Walter — *Wilson's Eskdale and Liddesdale Directory and Almanac for 1887*, Walter Wilson, High Street, Langholm 1887.

WRIGHT, Gordon — *MacDiarmid, An Illustrated Biography of Christopher Murray Grieve*, Gordon Wright Publishing, Edinburgh 1977.

LANGHOLM

In relation to this book

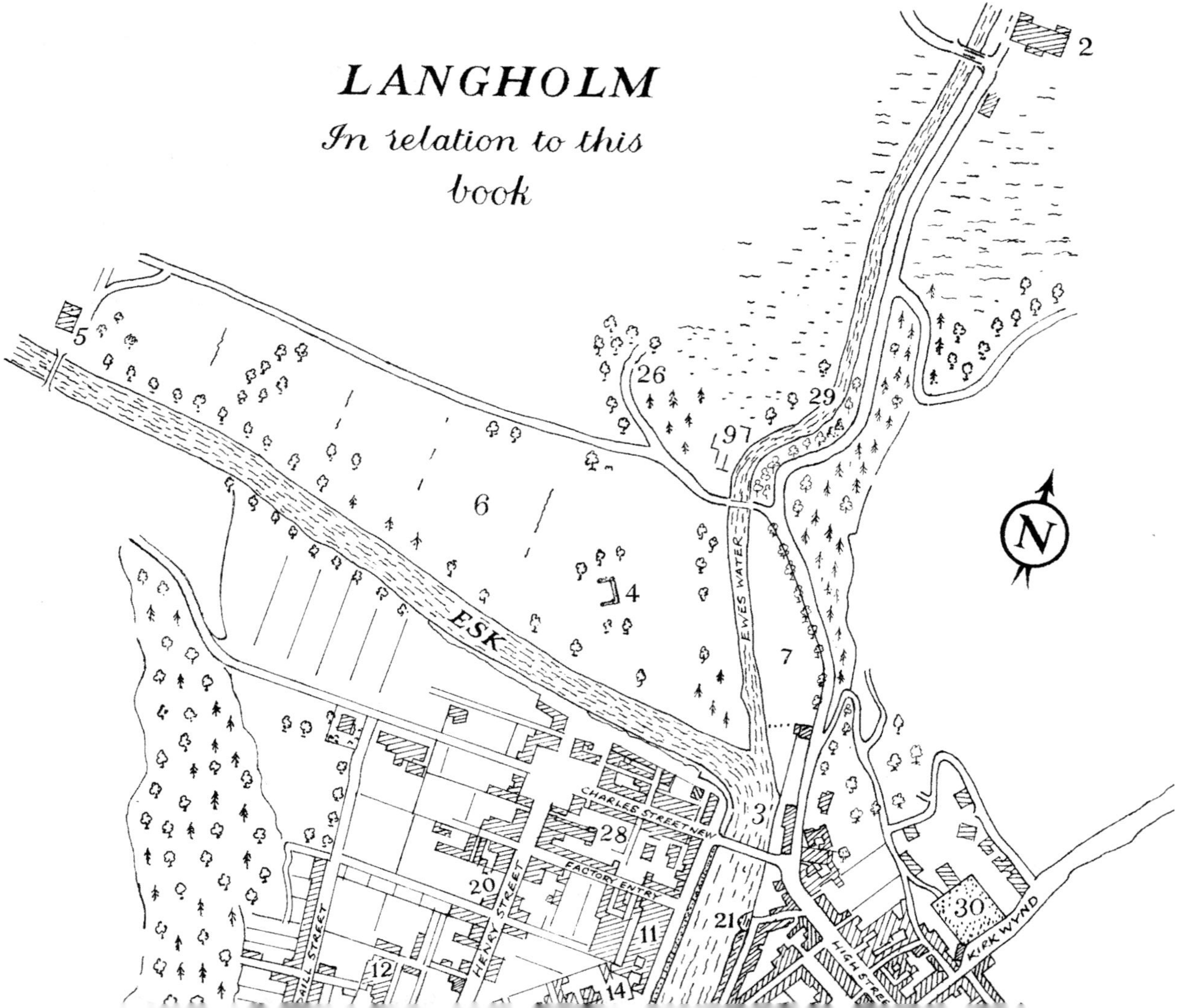

N

EWES WATER

ESK

HIGH STREET

KIRK WYND

CHARLES STREET

FACTORY END

HENRY STREET

MILL STREET

2

30

29

26

6

7

3

4

5

28

20

21

11

12

14